Early English Drama:
New Research in Archives, Authorship, and Performance

Published sumultaneously in Canada.
Printed in the United States of America.

ISBN-13: 978-0-9919760-4-1
ISBN-10: 0-9919760-4-5

Contents

The Medieval and Renaissance Drama Society (MRDS)

The Medieval and Renaissance Drama Society is an academic association of scholars, artists, and other individuals interested in Medieval and Renaissance drama. The Society's activities include organizing annual meetings, sponsoring long-range research projects, and publishing material of interest to the membership. The annual journal ROMARD, and the Early European Drama in Translation Series (EEDTS) are publications affiliated with MRDS. The MRDS business meeting is held annually each May at the International Congress on Medieval Studies at Western Michigan University in Kalamazoo, Michigan. Members and non-members are invited to attend. Each year MRDS sponsors conference sessions at the Medieval Congress in Kalamazoo, the Modern Language Association Convention, and the Medieval Congress in Leeds, England.

MRDS members receive the Society's Newsletter twice a year and the annual issue of ROMARD. To join MRDS, please visit the Society's website (http://themrds.org/membership) or contact the MRDS Secretary/Treasurer Frank Napolitano at fnapolitano@radford.edu. Dues Structure: Regular Member (US $25); Student (US $10); Friend (US $50); Benefactor (US $100).

About ROMARD

ROMARD wishes to thank Western University for its support through the Scholarly Journals at Western program.

ROMARD (ISSN 0098-647X) was published annually at Western University (London, Ontario). Starting with issue 58, the journal will be published by Medieval Institute Publications (Kalamazoo, MI). Inquiries concerning publication and the submission of articles should be submitted to the incoming Chief Editor, Kyle A. Thomas, at kathomas@missouristate.edu.

For all subscription inquiries, including institutional subscriptions and back issue orders, please contact orders@isdistribution.com.

Introduction

Robert L. A. Clark
Guest Editor

By a happy coincidence this volume, the last to be published under Mario Longtin's editorship of *ROMARD*, assembles five articles that are all devoted to the English medieval and early modern theater. The approaches taken by the authors are quite varied—ranging from archival research to textual analysis to authorship attribution—but they also offer a good deal of overlap. For example, the first three essays focus on material from transitional periods in English musical and dramatic practice. James Stokes documents changes in the "musical landscape" that occurred after the dissolution of the monasteries and ensuant changes in patronage, while Alan C. Dessen's article and the contribution by Dana Key and Emma Whipday both address the survival of allegory at a time when this mode of representation was going out of fashion. A further similarity is that three of the articles (Dessen, Key and Whipday, and Hubert) draw on what Key and Whipday term "practice as research," incorporating into their methodology the staging or reading of their respective texts and audience response to these performances. In Brian Vicker's article, on the other hand, detailed textual analysis is complemented by the use of digital technology in the form of anti-plagiarism software.

In "Waits, Other Musicians, and the Performance Tradition (Including Drama) in Early Suffolk," James Stokes draws on his research for the *REED: Suffolk* volume to document in rich detail his opening assertion that "the county was awash in music, whether performed by civic waits, household musicians, minstrels, fiddlers, pipers, blind harpers, drummers, or other music-makers variously identified by their skill with every instrument of the time." Stokes traces shifts in terminology and practice from the late thirteenth to the mid-seventeenth century as reflected in records ranging from those kept by towns to those of monastic and noble houses. Among the striking details that emerge from the rich tapestry of evidence is the career of blind Harry, a youth taken on as an apprentice by the Aldeburgh waits and whose association with them spanned more than twenty years.

As mentioned above, three essays in the volume integrate into their discussion stagings or readings of the plays they analyze. In his essay, "Residual Allegory in Elizabethan Drama: The One-Scene Psychomachia and Arresting the Vice," Alan C. Dessen focuses on the two types of stage action designated in his title, both of which draw on structures that were commonly used in allegorical representation. Workshop performances of nine scenes from allegorical and post-allegorical plays staged at the University of Toronto in 2010 sought to explore, in the words of director Peter Cockett, "an alternative way to understand the character's struggles" through the use of "an 'allegorical style' that is recognizably not Realism." Such scenes, according in Dessen, show "the persistence of allegory in English plays of the 1560s and 1570s at a time when the use of allegorical characters was no longer a dominant mode of representation."

In "*Tom Tyler and His Wife*: Allegory, Satire, Shrews and Sheep," Dana L. Key and Emma Whipday also focus on the transition between the medieval morality play tradition and the emerging social satire characteristic of the early modern genres of domestic comedies, shrew-taming plays, and city comedies. *Tom Tyler and His Wife* features allegorical characters such as Desire, Destiny and Patience alongside such recognizable types as the "authoritative wife" and the "cowardly husband." Key and Whipday also use a staged reading of the play, allowing them to gauge audience reaction to the beating of the wife by a brutal neighbor who, they note, "lacks the marital right to strike her." In their analysis, *Tom Tyler and His Wife* emerges as a sophisticated—and disturbing—exploration of sexual violence and gender politics in the pre-Shakespearean theater.

Ann Hubert's "*Amplificatio* in Performance: The Digby *Conversion of St. Paul* on Stage," which is partly informed by a student performance of the play at the University of Illinois at Urbana-Champaign, explores how *amplificatio,* a rhetorical technique of classical oratory and medieval preaching, serves as "a new rhetorical lens through which to understand the play's thematic and didactic engagement with pride and humility." In Hubert's reading, Saul becomes a "rhetorical tool of amplification"—a technique that he uses in the sermon that concludes the play. *Amplificatio* is thus shown to be "a rhetorical technique validating the conversion Saul undergoes."

In the last essay of the volume, Brian Vickers takes up the disputed authorship of *Arden of Faversham.* A response to a piece published by MacDonald Jackson in *Research Opportunities in Medieval and Renaissance Drama* in 2008, Vickers's article argues against Jackson's long-held opinion that Thomas Kyd was not the author of the play. Vickers takes a two-pronged approach to advance his position that Kyd was indeed the author. First, he uses recently developed anti-plagiarism software to compare word sequences in *Arden of Faversham* against language in the canon of plays definitely attributed to Kyd, finding a "deep affinity between *Arden of Faversham* and Kyd's three accepted plays at the level of phraseology." Vickers then turns to the dramaturgy of the play, specifically the sequential occurrence of "verbal ideas" in a given character's reaction to a situation, concluding that the combination of word sequences and dramaturgical likeness provides strong evidence that Kyd is indeed the author of *Arden of Faversham*.

The editors hope that the broad range of subject matter and analytical approach of the volume show off the dynamism of pre-modern theater studies.

Waits, Other Musicians, and the Performance Tradition (Including Drama) in Early Suffolk

James Stokes

The collected records of Suffolk give the considerable impression that, during the medieval and early modern periods, the county was awash in music, whether performed by civic waits, household musicians, minstrels, fiddlers, pipers, blind harpers, drummers, or other music-makers variously identified by their skill with every instrument of the time. But if the records describe a rich mosaic of musical performers, they also create a mosaic of confusion as to who these performers precisely were and what their performances involved. The terms used to describe both performer and performance evolved over time, and as the decades passed, a term such as "minstrel," for example, might give way to "musician," in the common usage. The term "play" might mean musical performance or drama. Local musicians played in an array of complex social, ceremonial, customary, and even judicial contexts, and one sometimes wonders if the records are making hierarchical or taxonomic distinctions whose nuances are lost to the modern ear. It may be that the range of contributions by musicians, particularly to drama and its related forms, has been under-estimated. Now that I have finished collecting the surviving records of drama, music, custom, and ceremony up to 1642 for the forthcoming volume, *REED: Suffolk*, it is possible to draw some conclusions concerning musicians in early Suffolk. The purpose of this study is to report that evidence concerning Suffolk musicians and the nature of their contributions particularly as they relate to drama and other mimetic forms. The essay begins with a consideration of waits, then moves to musical performers of other kinds. Because the identity of waits as troupes is so tied to towns, the discussion below proceeds by town. However, because the matter of other musicians involves so many additional factors, the discussion of those musicians in the second half of the article will proceed by a different organizing principle, described below.

The records show that Suffolk waits were, in most respects, typical. They had civic patrons. They functioned as companies controlled by a master. The towns hired the master and he, in turn, hired and paid the members of his company. Generally, the company performed as a troupe within the ceremonial and customary life of the town, but individual members, most often the master, might sometimes perform, and be paid, alone. The company might also travel to perform elsewhere entrepreneurially, as permitted by the town. The records often include details concerning the company's livery, wages, instruments, names, and rise or fall (as individuals and troupes). With the decline of traveling companies and their patrons during the late sixteenth and early seventeenth centuries, towns became a more stable patron for performers than were powerful lords in earlier times; while individual waits might come and go, troupes of waits often enjoyed a long tenure, secure in the musical monopoly provided by their patron town.

In spite of the relative wealth of detail concerning waits, unanswered questions as to the range of their kinds of performance persist. Did they only play music? Did they also sometimes perform as or with actors in productions? The common view concerning waits is that the former is true. However, some of the Suffolk records—particularly concerning the Ipswich waits—indicate otherwise. Waits in Ipswich can be found performing in drama.

The records show that at least six Suffolk towns (Aldeburgh, Bungay, Bury, Dunwich, Ipswich, and Walberswick) had performers whom they called waits. The earliest reference to a wait occurs in Walberswick; the most copious, detailed information occurs in Ipswich. For the other four towns known to have waits, the few references that survive provide but a fragmentary picture of the tradition in that town. Further, many communities and guilds retained one or more minstrels of their own, who functioned much as waits did (performing at feasts, dinners, and ceremonies, leading processions, receiving a wage), though they are not called waits in the records. For example, in Creeting St. Mary, the Jesus and Corpus Christi Guild retained its own minstrels. In 1468, the guild included two of those minstrels in its list of members. In 1496–97, the guild paid the minstrel Hart, and the (unnamed) taborer 12d. In 1500–01, the guild agreed to pay "the minstrel" a yearly wage of 12d to help the "holder" (presumably the holder of the banner?), and the holder was, in turn, to pay the minstrel an additional 12d yearly, plus the minstrel's costs. Thereafter, in nearly every year between 1501 and 1538, the guild accounts in Creeting St Mary include customary payments to the minstrel and to the bearer of the banner, and once, in 1535–36, to the singers as well. In 1524–25, Thetford Priory paid 12d to the minstrel of Wangford (It*e*m sol*uti* le menstrell of wa*n*gford xij d.). The wording sounds like a recognition of the minstrel's position. So, a great many Suffolk guilds and communities served as patrons to minstrels who carried out wait-like duties, though they might not be called by that name.

Aldeburgh

The first certain reference to the Aldeburgh waits occurs in 1573–74 (though a possible first reference occurs in 1567–78), and entries in the records continue thereafter through 1584–85. In 1581–82, the waits performed at the Christmas Court in Aldeburgh, and a payment for their dinner in 1583–84 confirms that the company of waits in Aldeburgh numbered four. Two of Aldeburgh's waits were certainly Peter Hunt and Thomas Brown. The third member of the company may have been John Brown, a minstrel whom the town paid in 1567 for fixing the clock and the dial, and other work, at the church. The fourth of the waits may have been John Bettes (later found among the Ipswich waits), who contributed to the care of a blind boy who would eventually become a wait. Drummers (and their apprentices), who may or may not have had an association with the waits, figure large in Aldeburgh's watches, musters, and training days between 1575–76 and 1642, continuing to appear in the records long after payments to the waits cease.

Numerous of the payments made to the Aldeburgh waits occur in connection with their care and training of Blind Harry, a boy whom the waits developed as one of their own, and who grew to be a respected musician in the town. The waits' involvement with Blind Harry spans more than twenty years in the records. The story begins with a family named Brown. In 1567, the town paid the above-mentioned minstrel, John Brown, for several tasks—fixing the clock and the dial, and his work at the church. In that same year, the town paid for stages and for a performance by the Queen's players. In 1572, the town sent a blind boy to a Mr. Brown (no first name), and the town otherwise paid for his care that year. The account for 1573–74 includes a variety of payments for the boy (thereafter identified as Harry): britches, shoes, a shirt, and his lodging for nine weeks in the care of Thomas Smith's wife. Eventually in that year, Harry was received into the care of Thomas Brown, one of the town's waits, a person likely related to John Brown, the minstrel, thereby creating the blind boy's first recorded encounter with the waits.

In the following year, 1575–76, the town paid the musician Peter Hunt "for taking blind Harry" as his apprentice and paid for a bed for the child. The town also paid Brown the wait (presumably Thomas) 26s 8d for "blind harrie," but whether for earlier care or for musical training is unclear. In either event, Harry had landed in the midst of a musical circle in Aldeburgh. In 1578–79, Blind Harry received 2 shillings from the town, so he must already have been performing by that time, and the town further paid for a coat, a pair of britches, a shirt, and a pair of hose. Harry must have proved to be extremely talented because in the next year, 1579–80, the town purchased for him a shalme and a viol, cases for the instruments, and another coat. In each of the next two years (1580–81 and 1581–82) the town paid him 16s, a set amount for what must have been either specific performances or an annual wage. During this decade, the town made separate payments to Harry and to the waits. Whether he was also taking part in the waits' performances at the town's courts is unclear, but his special relationship with the town continued. They paid for another coat in 1583–84. Two years later, they paid him 2s, and in 1587, they gave him 40 shillings to buy two more musical instruments. In 1591–92, they paid him 25s—presumably for a performance. It was his final appearance in the records. His recorded relationship with the town had spanned at least 20 years (perhaps much longer). The town's care had transformed a blind boy into a valued musician.

The Aldeburgh waits performed in the midst of both a local theatrical tradition and a visiting professional one. In 1582–83, officials paid 5s 8d to "the Players." In the same accounting year, the burgesses also ordered three separate payments for making and painting the devil's coat, which would seem to indicate a character in a morality play. Based on the terminology used to describe them, and the surrounding entries in the records, these players appear to have been a local troupe of amateur actors staging a play. The civic accounts include another reference to local players in September 1585. Between 1566–67 and 1634–35, numerous professional troupes with important patrons also performed in Aldeburgh, among them Norfolk's, Queen's (6 times), Leicester's (4 times), Bath's, Sheffield's, Howard's, Arundel's (twice), Essex's, Sussex's, King's (twice), and one unidentified troupe. The records identify only two venues where the plays were staged. In 1573–74, Leicester's Men performed in the church, and in the same year (and same page of the accounts), the town paid one Robert Lettes for going to men's houses to bid them "come to ffremans to the play." The records give no indication that the waits contributed to any of the local or the professional performances, though they did perform at the Lord's Court in 1579–80, and the Christmas Court in 1581–82.

Bungay

In 1443, the prioress of Bungay Priory paid 4d to a minstrel who occupied the position of wait in Bungay for an entertainment before her ("Et dat*i* cuid*a*m ministrallo ocup*anti* officiu*m* de le wayte in Bungey ad vnu*m* interludu*m* cora*m* d*omi*na monstrat*um*"). It is the earliest reference to a local wait in Suffolk, and the only reference to a wait in Bungay. The town had an extraordinary parish playing tradition stretching at least to the beginning of the fifteenth century.

In 1406–07, the Prioress of Bungay Priory had paid 6d to players from Bungay ("dat*i* ludentib*us* de Bungeye p*er* d*omi*ne vj d"). Sixteenth-century churchwardens' accounts contain uniquely copious detail concerning a scaffold play (also called a game) and church ale in Bungay. None of the surviving records mention the waits or other musicians as contributing to those productions.

Bury

The Bury waits first appear in the records in 1537–38, one year before the dissolution of the Abbey of Bury St Edmunds, when they received 12d for an appearance at Thetford Priory. At that point, they disappear from the records until the first half of the seventeenth century, during which period they appear in various civic records as regularly paid servants of the town. In 1621, the feoffees of the Town Lands Trust paid for the waits' liveries (sum missing), and in 1622/23 paid 3li 7d for blue cloth for their liveries and 54s 6d for their silver cognizances. The records show that in most years the waits performed at the feoffees' feasts, dinners, elections, and investitures. In 1617/18, they received 20s for wine and music when the new alderman took his oath, as they did in 1620/21, plus an additional 14s 3d that same year when the alderman took his place. In 1622/23, the feoffees paid the waits for performing at two dinners.

One of the Bury waits certainly appears to have been "Iohn Grene the Musitian," who was paid 10s at the feast when the new alderman took his oath in 1619/20 and received a like amount in 1621/22. The wills of two other resident musicians (William Allgate and Robert Hobart, who died respectively in 1642 and 1644) survive, but whether the two also served as waits the records do not say. During this same half-century, students from Bury School regularly performed plays, orations, and verses before the feoffees, and some evidence indicates that the waits may have contributed music to the scholars' efforts. The first recorded comedy by the boys (no mention of the waits) occurred in 1601. In 1607, one of the boys made an oration. In 1608, a list of charges for the scholars' play included a payment of 10s to the aforesaid John Green (his usual fee) "for his Musick at the Commodye." Since the event included a banquet, it is unclear whether Green's performance had to do with the play or the dinner, or both. The scholars twice performed verses for the assembled in 1609, and in 1639 the scholars acted a comedy before the High Sheriff of Suffolk, which required the making of a stage at the Abbey (the feoffees ordered that the stage be kept and used by the school). The records of neither event mention participation by the waits. The town also made considerable money in many years between 1604/05 and 1620/21 by renting out the guild hall for marriage dinners, but none of those entries in the accounts mentions performances by the waits or other musicians, though surely there would have been music.

Historically, Bury and its environs provided a rich musical environment, ranging from the Abbey, to Hengrave Hall and other nearby communities, to the town of Bury. The town had always chaffed against the abbey's control, and support for its troupe of waits reflects the town's growing civic identity.

Dunwich

In spite of eventually fatal erosion and decline at the hands of the sea, Dunwich strove to maintain its identity as a town through the early decades of the seventeenth century, exemplified by its company of waits. In its hiring of particular waits, however, the town did succeed in maintaining some measure of continuity. In 1601–02, the assembly ordered that the wait Thomas Copping and his company (including the wait, Robert Aleyn) should thereafter

> serue & keepe the s*ai*d watche w*i*th his instrument*es* by himself & S*er*vant*es* from & after the Mondaie next [after] after Mich*ael*mas daye last past vntill the ffeast of the Purification of St Mary the virgi*n* than next ensewing Saving onely for the tyme & vtys of Christmas./

Copping and Alyen were also listed as two of the 24 burgesses of the town at the assembly held on 23 December 1603. But in 1607–08, the town elected Thomas Thomplinson

> to be the waight of this o*u*r said towne and burghe and execute that place for one yere from Michaellmas next and that he shall haue twoe more of his Companye at the least accordingly as in tymes past hath ben vsed/

The order appears to confirm that companies of waits in Dunwich traditionally had 3 or more musicians. In 1609–10, the town paid one Edmund Crispe 8s for escutcheons for the waits. In 1613–14, the town named the waits James Rogers and Thomas Wootton to serve as assessors of common fines for the town, and the following year, in 1614–15, Rogers, Wootton, and their company were chosen to be the town's waits. Thereafter, the waits (like the town itself) faded permanently away.

Walberswick

The records of Walberswick contain only four references to their wait, all from the late fifteenth century, but theirs is the second earliest recorded tradition of waits (after Bungay) in Suffolk. In 1469–70, the Walberswick churchwardens paid 16d "to the Wayte for to sette þe clerk for his labour." The wording is obscure, but the previous entry in the accounts says, "It*e*m for wode to þe clerk*es* hegge and making ther of 3s 2d." The two entries indicate work being done on behalf of the clerk, some of it by the wait. In 1482, the wardens paid the wait 2d "for ij chywys" (meaning obscure), and in 1595–96, the wait received 4d from the wardens "for the hows," again presumably indicating work done for the parish. Finally, in 1596–67, the wardens gave 2s "to the wayte a Reward," which sounds very much like payment for a performance. These few entries indicate that Walberswick retained at least one wait during the late fifteenth century, and that he worked for the parish as both an entertainer and a laborer.

Walberswick had robust festive and customary traditions in which the contributions of the wait would have proved useful. The parish had innumerable ales, some of which (May ales, maidens' ales, wives' ales, and young men's ales) had mimetic and/or musical elements. For example, Walberswick had its own game (play), held with a church ale in 1492–93, and held another ale in either 1493–94 or 1494–95 (depending on how one reads the records). Two other communities (Bramfield and Wenhaston) showed their games in Walberswick, presumably meaning that they cried the banns of their own game there; and Blythburgh brought its May to Walberswick. Walberswick itself attended ales and made contributions to them in at least five other communities (Blythburgh, Halesworth, Rumburgh, Southwold, and Yoxford). The parish had processions, for which the maidens held a gathering for torches in 1487–88. In parishes elsewhere, musicians often led processions of that kind, so it may be reasonable to think that they did so here. However, the laconic records do not make it possible to confirm that the Walberswick wait did indeed participate in any of those activities.

Ipswich

By far the most detailed picture of waits in Suffolk occurs in the Ipswich records. Between 1296 and 1530, various kinds of musicians turn up in the civic records, but none of them are identified as waits. Although a city of the importance of Ipswich may well have had waits in earlier centuries, civic accounts from medieval Ipswich, where payments to waits might have been expected to appear, do not survive. The city made the first documentable payment to its waits on 4 November 1538 when it granted an annual wage of 13s 4d to each member of a company of three waits. Thereafter, regular annual payments to waits begin to appear in 1565–66, the point at which surviving Elizabethan accounts in Ipswich commence.

During the Elizabethan and Stuart years, successive troupes of waits enjoyed stable, long-term employment with the city. The first of those troupes, serving between 1561 and 1582, included the master wait, William Martin, and his company of musicians. From the records, it appears that the town hired

Martin, and (given the large amounts awarded) that he in turn hired the musicians in his company. Martin first appears in the records in 1561–62, when he received 5s on Corpus Christi Day. He next appears on 7 December 1565 when he received 13s 4d for his service at the previous meeting of The Guild (feasts, elections, and investitures usually referred to in the records as "the guild"). In that same year he received another 5s for his music at the guild. On 8 December 1566 he received the same amount, plus the award thereafter of an annual wage of 20s. On 4 June 1567, he again received 10s for his music at the guild, as he did on 12 July 1568." Up to this point, the records name only Martin when awarding payments for his music, but on 24 September 1567, the burgesses ordered that the town's waits should receive liveries and cognizances. In the account for 1568–69, the town authorized liveries and scutcheons for five waits. In that same year, the town awarded 10s "to Martyn the mynstrell for him & his company in playing before Mr Bayliff*es* at there entry of the baylywick." Another time that year, they paid Martin 5s "for playing before Mr Baylye Whetcroft at his going to Michaelmas terme."

Two entries in the records indicate that this company of waits also performed as actors. In 1568–69, they received 10s "for playing the ffooles in the halle," and in 1571–72, the town paid 6s 8d "To will*ia*m Martyne & his companye for a plaie at the Mote hall." The entries provide rare confirmation that waits sometimes performed as actors in addition to providing music.

In each year between 1572 and 1582, the town paid William Martin 10s for performing on what was variously called "the guild day," "the guild," or "the guild dinner." In 1572–73, the payment specifically included "Martyne & his companye for ther musick at þe yeld." In 1575–76, his annual payment of 10s refers to him also as "Clarke of the Markett." The account for that year indicates that in addition to the 10s paid him as wait, he also received 6s 8d in wages each quarter as Clerk of the Market. So his entrepreneurial skills extended well beyond music. In 1582, Martin and his company of five other musicians appeared in the records for the final time on 6 April, when the town ordered that

> Will*ia*m Marten & his Company being 6 in all shall have waight*es* [pipes] bought at the Townes Chardge & that he & they shall therwith *ser*ue the Towne for one yere in suche order as by the bayliff*es* shalbe thought mete & requisit And the said Will*ia*m & his Company to stand to the considerac*i*on of the Towne for ther Wages in that behalf, And it is furder agreed by the consent of the said Will*ia*m that if the Towne shall not lyke of ther *ser*uice at the yeres ende that then he the said Will*ia*m shall repaye the so*m*me of mony the Towne shall so disburse backe ageyne And for the better assurance of payment therof the said Wil*lia*m p*ro*miseth to stonde bound With sufficient suerties accordyngly as by Mr Bayliff*es* for the tyme being shall thinke mete and allowe of/.

Subsequently in 1582, Martin either died or retired and his company seemingly disbanded.

Then began the brief tenure of Thomas Keele and his company. The short stay of Keele's company in the records suggests that they were, at best, an interim group, while the council found a permanent replacement for Martin. On 22 March 1583, the council ordered that

> ffower p*er*sons meete for waits shall be retained in the Towns service, as by the Bayliff for the time beeing shall be ordered, and they shall have 4 pounds from the Towne, beside theire common collection, and every of them a livery at the Towns charge. And for theire last yeres service they shall have 40s.

In 1583–84, and again in 1584–85, the council approved liveries for the four waits. In 1585–86, the town paid 6s 8d "to Thomas Keele & his company for musicke at the Guylde." In that same year, in response to a request by Sir Francis Walsingham, knight, the town ordered that the "Musitians of this Towne" (presumably still Keele's company) should have 4li in wages annually and retain the right to collect benevolences from the town:

> wheras request is made by l*ett*res fro*m* S*i*r ffraunc*i*s walsingha*m* knight aswell touching the Musitians wages of this Towne, dewe this yere by the Towne as also [fos] for the colleccion of the benevelenc of the Inh*ab*itant*es* of this Towne, yt is Agred that they shall haue ther wages being iiij li dewe by the Towne paid to the*m* & for the rest co*m*myng of the benevolenc of the [Towne] Inh*ab*itant of the Towne they shall collect that them selues / And yt is furder agred that they shall not be chardged w*i*th x s delyu*er*d to ballard nor w*i*th viij s paid for his herse hyer to lende, nor to v s geven to the p*er*syvant who [illegible word] for the said Musitc*i*ons.

Keele and his men thereafter disappear from the Ipswich records.

John Bettes, who came after Keele, served 20 years (1587–1607), far longer than any previous master wait in Ipswich. It seems likely that Bettes had previously served as a wait in Aldeburgh. In 1579–80, that town of Aldeburgh had advanced John Bettes 10s "to bye blynd harry a Coat." Harry was the blind youth taken as an apprentice by the Aldeburgh waits. Seven years later, on 20 October 1587, the Ipswich council ordered that

> Iohn Bett*es* musitian with his companye to the nomber of ffore p*er*sons shall Inioye the offyce of the weyght*es* within this Towne to s*er*ue in that offyce ffrom the daye of the date herof vntyll assensc*i*on daye next & that they shall p*ro*cede ther about*es* nightlye from two of the Clock vntyll they have gone throughout the Towne And further that they shalbe at the co*m*mandement of the Towne duryng the whole yere for furder s*er*uice in ther musyck and

> therrbye it is agreed that they shall haue for ther salarye & wages this yere iiij li. & convenyent lyveryes of the Townes Chardge & besydes receyve the benevolence of the Inh*ab*itant*es* of the Towne As Iohn Marten the late musition[.] hertofore have vsed to collect the same p*ro*uided it is agreed that the said wayt*es* shall prouide the*m* ther cognizanc*es* of ther owne charg[.]e.

Throughout all his years of service to the town, Bettes and his company received that same annual fixed amount of 4li and livery costs, plus the right to collect additional money from audiences. On the same day that Bettes was first named as wait in 1587, the town elected John Cressey (alias Mynter) Drummer of the Town, to receive 20s and livery costs each year. Thereafter, he performed together with the waits many times in civic ceremonials.

In 1588–89, Bettes and a co-partnering wait, Raffe Owenden (elsewhere Oldham), together received 12s from the town toward their liveries. On 2 November 1590, the council ordered that

> the musitions & wayt*es* of this Towne shall contynewe in ther offic*es* this yere accordyng to ther former retayner for such wag*es* lyveris & ffees as heretofore hathe ben allowed them and that they shall have ffrom henceforth tyll the feast of the Anunciac*i*on of our lady next & so forthe this yere as Mr baliff*es* for the Tyme being shall thinke mete And in Consideraci*o*n therof it is agreed that if they have a fyfte man into ther Company that then ffyfte man shall also have a lyvery only as the other, Provided it is agreed tht Iohn Bett*es* & Rauff oldh*a*m shalbe only masters of ther company aforsaid & have the Ioynt Gou*er*nement of the rest of ther company.

Thereafter, Bettes and Oldham were both named when the company received its wages in 1592–93, 1593–94, 1594–95, and 1596–97. After that year, Oldham disappears from the records.

Bettes's company, like that of William Martin earlier, contributed to dramatic productions, though whether as actors the documents do not say. All the evidences of the waits and drummers' possible involvement in staging relate to the commemoration of the Queen's Coronation, an event held annually on 17 November. In 1562–63, expecting a visit from the young queen, the town had prepared speeches and ordered repairs, but the visit never happened and the town rescinded those orders. The first recorded celebration of the Queen, and her Coronation, dates from 1578, the year in which she actually visited Ipswich. The annual celebration continued thereafter until 1600.

The event itself commemorating the Queen's Coronation certainly included drama, pageantry, speeches, and shows. In September 1578, the Council paid the scrivener, John Kynge, 6s 8d for charges related to the pageant he had made, and 40s for "setting forthe of pagent*es* aswell at þe yeld [the guild day] as Ageinst the quenes Comynge." In the following year (1578–79), Kynge again supplied "the pagent At the guild," receiving 2li 4s 8d for his efforts, and Will*ia*m Marten received 10s "for his musike at the Guylde," though whether pageant and music were involved in a single production the records do not confirm.

The commemoration of the Coronation may have lapsed between 1579 and 1582 because the records grow silent during those three years, but on 19 December 1582, the council ordered that

> Wheras Iohn Kynge scolemaster in the xvii ten daye of november last wherin the Quenes ma*ies*ties reigne newly beganne ageyne was at Charge about certen pageant*es* & other Shewes in this Towne in Ioye of that daye. Item agreed that he shall have geven to him out of the Towne Treasur in full satisfacc*i*on of & for his said Charges & paynes taken in that behalf fourty shilling*es* to be payd by the Threasyur.

In 1582–83, the Treasurer gave "Iohn Kinge the Screuener" what appears to be a late payment for the same pageants and shows of 2li "for his Chardges of his pagent*es* made on the Quenes Daye the 17en of November / 1582." In that same year (1582–83), the treasurer's account also rewards Kynge 3li 6s 8d "for his shewes & speches at the Gylde daye." If these two John Kings were one and the same (and clearly they were), then he was both the schoolmaster and a scrivener. In 1583, John King received five marks for having

> lately made shewe of a certen pageant in forme of a Shippe with certen convenynt speches therin At the last Guylde m*er*chant holden within the Towne at his owne Chardges [he] shalbe therfore allotted toward*es* his said Chardg*es* in that behalf ou*er* & besyd*es* suche mony as he hath receyued alredy of the aldermen of the said Guylde ffyve mark*es* out of the Townes Treasure.

The entry indisputably connects pageantry and drama in the Ipswich celebrations.

Kynge appears in the records a final two times in 1583–84. In that year, the Treasurer paid 3li 6s to "King screwener for charges of his pagente by warrant As Apereth by great Court." The Order Book of the Great Court contains this decision relative to that warrant:

> for Iohn Kyng*es* petic*i*on touching his demaund for allowance of his Charg*es* at a shewe made on the coronac*i*on daye last in this Towne shalbe considred vppon & ordered by Mr Bailiff*es* that now ben & Mr Bayliff*es* newe elect & by them to be allowed as they or the most of them shalbe thought good.

At this point, Kynge and the City had a parting of the ways. It was the last such payment to Kynge. In that same year (1583–84), during the same period of time when Kynge was producing his usual show, the city paid a new schoolmaster, one Mr. Smythe, 40s for preparing an oration on the Coronation Day. The fact that the Great Court was responding to Kynge's "demaund" for payment is perhaps telling, and that he was paid by warrant indicates that he was now an outsider. In any event, Kynge appears in the records no more. It was apparently Kynge, not the waits, who made the Coronation show possible. When he disappears, so does the Coronation celebration for three years, during the temporary tenure of the wait Thomas Keele and his company.

These and other entries through the years confirm that Kynge customarily made pageants, speeches, and shows for two different events (the Coronation Day and the Guild Day) each year. In the aggregate, the content of these entries suggests that the event on Coronation Day, in dramatic terms, had included at the least a rough blending of pageants and speeches, and perhaps something much more theatrically sophisticated. That these dramatic events occurred at "The Guild" and that the waits performed at "The Guild" increases the likelihood that the waits made contributions to drama in Ipswich during the late sixteenth century.

The beginning of the tenure of John Bettes and his company in 1587–88 coincides with the return of the Coronation Day celebration after its three-year absence from the records. In the year of their hire, Bettes's troupe received 6s 8d for "ther servis done one the Quens Daye." The wording suggests the possibility that their contribution that day involved more than music alone, since it also marks the return of the Ceremony. Another person, one Grenelefe, also received 1s 8d "for his paines taken the same day," as did John Mynter for his drumming.

In 1588–89, the council paid for paper and thread to bind up gunpowder to be used on Coronation Day and at a triumph on a different day. On 12 November, the council granted authority to procure a show and triumph for the next Coronation Day, so it does appear that the event on Coronation Day had taken, and would retain, a militaristic and patriotic turn; in that year, the event included the showing and training of the ordinary soldiers of the town. Entries in subsequent years show the same pattern concerning the commemoration of the Coronation: 87 pounds of gunpowder for the triumph and "Solemynysye" in 1590; speeches by youths in 1591–92; a show by Thomas Stevenson and speeches by scholars in 1595; and a speech by Mr Doweinge in 1599.

The celebration on Coronation Day still involved a play or some other performance at the end of the sixteenth century because on 29 December 1599, the town paid one William Allderton 3s for "4 fette for the tresselles & settinge them vpp with makinge of the stadge one the Queens day beinge the xvij of November iij s."

The celebration of the Coronation of the monarch disappears from the records between 1600 and 1632, although the town drummer was paid 1s 8d "at the show" in 1614–15. There is nothing in the records to indicate that this particular show involved Coronation Day. The celebration returns mid-reign in Charles I. References include payments to the musicians for playing on Coronation Day in 1632–33, 1633–34, 1634–35, and 1636–37. Thereafter, it is gone forever.

Bettes and his company continued to serve through 1607. Payments for their livery in 1603 name the four members of the troupe as John Bettes, Hugh Wakefield, Alexander Thomas, and John Allen. Other than this entry in 1603, the annual payments for the waits' wages recur with numbing consistency and lack of variation through 1607. For some reason, in 1607 the town paid Bettes's troupe through the end of the accounting year, then discharged them and refused them new liveries. The troupe had either decided to take itself to a new patron elsewhere or had run afoul of the town. In any event, Bettes died 29 years later, in Ipswich.

In 1608, the town hired a new troupe of 4 waits, for 5li annually, plus livery. In its order, the council agreed that

> Att this Assemblie Rob*er*t Caraweye Thomas Salter Thomas [Mud*es*] Mudd*es* & George Mudd*es* are reteyned to be music*ians* of this towne fro*m* o*ur* ladie [lac] last during one whole yere for v l A yere halfe yerelie to be p*ai*d & [a liverie] clothe for A liverie for eu*er*ie of them they to [playe] goe aboute the towne from hallowmas tell o*ur* ladie w*i*th there musicke as the former music*io*ns had w*i*th sackbutt*es* cornett*es* & A lute [And they to haue A lute in there companye], And the benevolence of the Inh*ab*itant*es* of this towne as haue ben vsed to the former music*ia*ns / And they to haue v of there Companye.

However, another payment (for livery cloth) in 1607–08 mentions six waits; and in 1609, the council names the six, its order saying that

> Att this Assemblie Thomas Salter Thomas Mudd*es* Alexander Thomas Thomas Burrag Symon Minds & [.]e Valentyne Wheyman [It is agreed that Thomas Salter & his Companye] are Reteyned to be music*io*ns of this towne to serue therein according to the Accustomed order during one yere to come soeas they be of good behavior & shall haue there Accustomed wag*es* & [Al] eu*er*ie one of them A lyverie coate Clothe for this yere to come / betwene viij s & x s the yard.

Entries in 1609–10 and 1610–11 also indicate that Salter was the master of the troupe. An order in 1611 names five of the same six waits, with only Valentyne Wheyman missing from the list. By October 1613, Salter has disappeared from the records, replaced by Burrage as master; and in 1613, the number of waits is again listed as five, but with the addition of a singing boy:

Att this Assemblye Thomas Burrag & Richard Lord & the rest of the Companye of musicians of this towne nowe being shall haue [paid them x] xiij li vj s viij d from Michaelmas last yerelie during ij yeres att our ladie & michaelmas by euen purcas for there wages And Afterward that they shall haue paid them xx li yerelie at the our ladie & michaelmas by euen purcas.

in consideracion whereof Thomas Burrag Richard Lord Alexander Thomas [Thomas] Iohn Stone Symon Mynes Musicians of the towne [hav] haue Agreed with A singing boye not [to goe] depart out of this towne with there musick without the license of þe Bayliffes And shalbe redie at all tymes [with there musick within the towne] to pleye vppon there Instrumentes [when they] within [the sam] this towne when they shalbe Required therevnto by the Bayliffes of þe towne for the tyme being /.

Burrage first came into the records in 1609 and served as master from 1613 through 1637, when waits stopped appearing in the records. According to his will, Burrage (identified in his will as a musician) died before 1 March 1669, when his will was proved. His will mentions no family or heirs. Burrage was the one constant during his 24 years as master of the waits. In 1614, the city agreed to retain for two years the same five waits and singing boy named in October 1613 (unless a boy with a better singing voice were found). Of the five waits, Burrage, Alexander Thomas, and Symon Mynes remained from the company of 1611; Richard Lowe and John Stone were new additions. The singing boy is not named. The fact that this order also specifies that the troupe is not to travel to perform beyond the city without a license from the bailiffs indicates that they likely did sometimes travel to perform. Their wages of 20li per year are quadruple what they had been a mere three years earlier.

In 1614–15, the drummer was paid "for one day at þe show" so the city was still sponsoring stagings of some kind, and indeed, in 1616–17, the city paid "for a tilt on the heathe," and "for a clothe to tilte withall," but whether the waits also participated the records do not say. In that same year, the city reduced the wages of the waits proportionally because one of their number, Symond Myndes, was discharged for unlawfully begetting two children:

[It is Agreed that] Att this Assemblye Symon Mynes [whoe] one of the musicians of this towne [shalbe] is dischardged from his place [for his that offence for his misbehavior] for that he hath vnlawfullie [hathe ben Accused with car being Accused by] begotten with two children one Alice Ward of whose bodye he confesseth he had the vse severall tymes [vnlawfullie] [to haue begotten her with with [dittography] child vnlawfullie, hathe confessed that whereof whoe hathe confessed that he haue had the vse of her bodie], And it is Agreed that he shall not be suffred herafter to be contynewe for one of the

Company of the musicians of this towne nor to weare the towne lyverie within this towne or in the company [of] of the said musicians or any of them.

However, he was reinstated a year later because in 1617–18, the city paid 15s "to make Symonde Myndes one of the Musitians A liuerye Coate."

Other Musicians

While waits never stopped being identifiable as waits and can be discussed by the towns who hired them, to consider other musical performers requires a more complex organizing principle. Terms used to identify these other musicians evolved over time and often overlapped in confusing ways. Further, patrons might range from towns, religious houses, gentry, members of the royal family, parishes, guilds (both craft and religious), innkeepers, and justices, to other individuals and institutions. Such a discussion needs to consider the kinds of performers and their shifting names, the range of patrons, and the differing performance situations (including drama, custom, and ceremony), all within a roughly chronological context.

Early Suffolk records occasionally use many terms to identify performers according to a particular skill (luter, harper, trumpeter, drummer, singer, etc.), but through the early sixteenth century the one constant in the records is the recurring appearance of the word "minstrel." The records seldom say precisely what it means (even the *REED Anglo-Latin Wordbook* defines "ministrallis" only as "entertainer"), but its ubiquitous occurrences in the records makes it possible to track its use and to derive some sense of its meaning(s).

The earliest reference to a musician in Suffolk is the reference to one Edric Vielator or fiddler, who rented one acre of land in mid-thirteenth century Bures (near Stoke-by-Nayland). The earliest reference to actual performances by minstrels (or any other kinds of performers) occurs in November and December 1296 and January 1297 in the household account books of Edward I. During that two-month period, Edward chose to celebrate, in Ipswich, the nuptials and wedding of his daughter and youngest child, Elizabeth Plantagenet, to John 1, Count of Holland. The king's progress into Suffolk brought with it a host of minstrels and other performers, including citharistas (lyrists) who performed on 20 November and 9 December 1296 at Bury and Bures respectively. In the King's Hall at Ipswich on 27 December, performer Matilda Makejoy danced before Lord Edward, fourth son of Edward I and the future Edward II. On 8 January 1297, the day of the couple's nuptials, the account book records payments to at least 40 performers, including seven named minstrels and diverse other minstrels, six lyrists, three videlators, two harpers, two trumpeters, a fool, a taborer, and at least 14 other performers either unnamed or having obscure designations of their talents. While these performers were not local in that most had royal or noble patrons and came temporarily into Suffolk with the king's household, their presence reflects an awareness of sophisticated musical and dramatic performance in Ipswich by the end of the thirteenth century. That these thirteenth-century references to performers occur in royal records only reflects the fact that those are, in general, the earliest records revelatory of performers to survive.

During the first half of the fourteenth century, Suffolk musicians turn up in state papers and in a fragmentary but performatively rich financial account from the Abbey of Bury St Edmunds. The state papers include Nicholas de Creeting, a taborer, who received a royal pardon in 1313, as did Roger of Bury, a harper, in 1322, and John Manpryne, the Abbot of Bury's minstrel, in 1337. In 1314, William de ffitheler (fiddler), described as the Abbot of Bury's man, received a pardon for assault. In 1348, Edward of Woodstock, The Black Prince, awarded a war horse to a minstrel in connection with a hastiludium (joust or tournament) held at Bury. During this half century, the Suffolk minstrels were apparently a roisterous lot.

The early fourteenth century record from the abbey is a parchment fragment of an abbey account for the year 1335–36 now bound into a compendium of ecclesiastical writings. This year was momentous for the Abbey, for Suffolk, and for the North, including a tournament at Newmarket (about 15 miles from Bury) and the holding of a parliament at York. Fortunately, the part of the account that survives happens to be the section headed "Gifts Given to Minstrels" (Dona dat' minstrall'). Under the single heading "'Minstrels," the entries include payments (all made on eight major feast days between All Saints 1535 and the Ascension of the Lord in 1536) to at least 25 minstrels (none of whose patrons are identified), plus a juggler, a harpist, a taborer, and 7 trumpets (all ten of whom had named patrons among the nobility). The fragment also includes payments to bearwards, royal heralds, messengers, and yeomen of the guard. In the mind of that particular scribe at Bury, the rubric "Minstrel" included all of those performers. For example, immediately after paying a juggler, a bearward, and his servant, the account lists a payment to what it calls "other minstrels" (a*ljs* menestrall*is*). Similarly, it then paid four trumpeters and "alijs menestrallis." This particular phrasing recurs throughout the payments. The inclusive meaning of the term "minstrel" in that year is confirmed by one entry in particular on this page, a payment at Christmas to a certain minstrel of the Earl of Northamptonshire, namely, a juggler (in Nat*alis* d*omi*ni cuid*em* menestrall*i* de Comit*is* Norhant vid*elice*t Tregettour). The account shows that at this moment in the early fourteenth century, the local landscape at Bury was littered with performers of almost every kind in an atmosphere mingling royalty, nobility, ecclesiastics, local gentry, and performers. The abbey was obviously a major host to performers.

During the second half of the fourteenth century, payments to minstrels and other music makers giving local sponsored performances emerge. All of those performances occurred at three religious houses (Mettingham College, the Abbey of Bury St Edmunds, and Ipswich Priory); many of the payments were made to performers whose patrons were members of the nobility. During the 1390s, Mettingham College in north-east Suffolk, where the greatest number of performances occurred, paid the minstrels of the lords Norfolk, Willoughby (three times), and Morley; the minstrels of the Lord Bishop (unnamed); the taborer of the Norfolk town of Gillingham; and several other unnamed minstrels and taborers. In 1387–88, Bury Abbey paid the minstrels of the Earl Marshall and of lord Norfolk. In 1360–61, Ipswich Priory awarded 8s to the minstrels of diverse lords (ministrall*is* diu*er*sor*um* d*omi*nor*um*). Except for taborers, all musical performers in these records, whether with patrons or without, are identified as minstrels.

During the fifteenth century, the number of musical performers in the records grows exponentially, with literally hundreds of musicians turning up in the increasingly copious records. Among religious houses, the registers of Mettingham College record payments to music-makers in nearly every year between 1400 and 1500. Abbey officials at Bury paid musicians intermittently throughout the century in nearly every account roll that survives. In 1443–44, at a play before the Prioress of Bungay Priory, her scribe recorded a payment of 4d given for his dwelling to a minstrel then holding the office of wait in Bungay (Et dat*i* cuid*a*m ministrallo ocup*anti* officiu*m* de le wayte in Bungey ad vnu*m* interludu*m* cora*m* d*omi*na monstrat*um* *pro* ten*emento* suo infra temp*us* Natal*e* d*omi*ni hoc A*nn*o iiij d). Whether the wait was performing in connection with the play is not clear from the entry (though it seems likely that he was). In 1497–98, Felixstowe Priory paid a citharedus (a lyrist accompanying himself with song) at their Christmas feast.

The sheer copiousness of fifteenth-century payments to musical and other performers in the Mettingham registers, and the more modest number of survivals in Bury St Edmunds's spottier records, offer insights into the contrasting ways in which religious houses in Suffolk supported entertainers during that century. Both religious foundations were major hosts to performers. At Mettingham, the pattern never substantially varies. Each year, the college paid both minstrels and other performers in great number. Between 1396 and 1536, it made 211 such payments to minstrels. Since the college paid both individual minstrels and troupes of minstrels with single amounts, the actual number of minstrels who performed is far greater than the 211 payments. During that same period, the college also paid lusores (39 times); taborers (22); citharedi (7);

bearwards and fools (4 each); boy bishops, jesters, salianti (dancers) and tumblers (2 times each); plus a luter, mimi (performers or waits), and a symphoniste (a musician) (all 1 time each). In paying performers, the Mettingham records always carefully distinguish between minstrels and those other performers, whether musical or not. In 14 instances, the registers record those minstrels being paid together with other performers (see final section of article).

Of the 211 payments to single minstrels or troupes at Mettingham, 184 went to minstrels whose patrons were members of the nobility or the monarchy—28 of them in all. The four noble patrons whose minstrels were paid most often all had local connections: Lord Willoughby (20 times), Lord Morley (15), the Dukes of Norfolk (14), and the Duke of Suffolk (12); the king's minstrels visited more than those of any other patron (19 times). Eight of the remaining patrons to minstrels included six towns, one diocese, and one unidentifiable place. Of the 211 payments to minstrels in the Mettingham registers, the remaining 19 mention no patron, either identifying the minstrel by name only or giving no indication of the minstrel's identity at all. Of the dated performances, 27 occurred at Christmas, four on the college's common day, one at Shrovetide, and one at Pentecost. Nearly all of those payments were to players only, or to minstrels and players together, and only rarely to minstrels only. None of the many other payments bear a specific date of performance other than the half year that the accounts often cover.

Before the time of Henry VIII, the Mettingham registers always describe the performers who had noble patrons as being minstrels. Lacking descriptive distinctions, it is impossible to know whether those minstrels were always musicians only or were sometimes actors as well, though the former appears more likely. The number of minstrels sponsored by a noble patron varied from one to an indeterminate several. These minstrels never demonstrably received payments for performing together with locals (though they may well have done so, especially at Christmas), although minstrels without noble patrons did do so (see final section of article). In the few cases when the college paid other kinds of performers with noble patrons, those performers (taborers, bearwards, dancers, and harpists) could never be mistaken for a troupe of actors. The one exception is the "mimi" of Lord Willoughby who could conceivably have been players. As alluded to above, the records make clear distinctions between minstrels and players. In the fourteenth century, those players were almost always called lusores, usually described as playing ("ludentes"). One entry at Shrovetide in 1468–69 (Item p*at*ri & filio lusorib*us* & ludentib*us* temp*or*e Carnibreuij iiij d) appears to distinguish between actors (the father and son) and another kind of player (ludentibus), perhaps performers in customary games or sports. Otherwise, lusore is the fifteenth century term of choice for actor in the Mettingham registers.

Because the Mettingham College records so consistently distinguish between minstrels and other performers (including players), the impression arises that in those records minstrels were always musicians. The word "minstrel" appears, in most cases, to have conveyed a measure of professional identity and a level of musical skill, especially in minstrels of the king, a nobleman, a town, or a diocese that warranted a patron's protection and ensured his or its satisfaction with the performer. Identifying minstrels, both solo and troupes, by name in payments appears to be an acknowledgment of their status or their skill, or their familiarity, for example: Nicholas, minstrel of Lord Willoughby in 1419–20; William Prentyng and his associate; and Nicholas Duk, minstrel of Lord Willoughby (perhaps the same minstrel as in 1419–20), both in 1421–22 (and Prentyng again in 1422–23); Nicholas Scarlet in 1463–64 and 1464–65; John Scarlet in 1486–87 and (with his associates) in 1488–89; William Scarlet in 1486–87 and 1487–88; and Thomas Scarlet in 1489–90 and 1490–91. Other named minstrels occur in the records through 1514–15. However, many other payments to minstrels include no identifying name. Unless minstrels were players in minstrels' clothing, no itinerant troupes of professional actors are confirmably recorded at Mettingham, though many troupes of local players are.

Fifteenth-century payments from Bury, though few in number, reveal a distinct pattern of performances spanning the century. In the surviving accounts, performances occur on three occasions each year: the ceremony of the Boy Bishop on the Feast of St Nicholas (8 December); the commemoration of St Edmund's Day (20 November), and the feast of Christmas. Abbey officials paid minstrels for performing in the hall in 1401–02, and a minstrel at Christmas in 1417–18. They paid the Boy Bishop in 1417–18, 1422–23, and 1493–94. And they rewarded minstrels on the Feast of St Edmund in 1417–18, 1429–30, and 1486–87. They also paid for "ollis" or "crusys" for the trumpeters in 1493–94. Bury resembles Mettingham College in the way it sponsors these performances on major feast days, notably at Christmas. But the fifteenth-century Abbey at Bury differs utterly from Mettingham in that its surviving accounts include absolutely no payments to local festive performers or unsponsored entertainers of other kinds. The fourteenth-century Abbey is much more insular and seemingly uninvolved with local custom than was Mettingham.

During this century, musical entertainers increasingly turn up in other kinds of records as well, notably the households of the nobility and the gentry. In 1402, Thomas de Mowbray, 4th earl of Norfolk, of Framlingham Castle, took into service the harper, Simon Huittbone. In 1408/09, a household account of Michael de la Pole, 2nd Earl of Suffolk, of Wingfield, includes a section called "ffeoda ministrall*is*," that is, a section of regular fees being paid to de la Pole's own entertainers, which included a trumpeter, a player of the bumbard, and two shalmosers or players of shawms. Another section of the same account (Gifts and Rewards) includes a payment to four minstrels of the Earl of Somerset. In 1412–13, an account of Dame Alice de Bryne of Acton Hall near Long Melford contains 15 payments to musicians between Christmas Day and 27 July in that accounting year (four of them to minstrels, ten to harpers, most of them between Christmas and Lent). Richest in musical entertainers among the nobility (both men and women) are the household accounts of Sir John Howard, first Duke of Norfolk, of Stoke-by-Nayland. Between 1462 and 1467 alone, he made eleven payments to troupes of minstrels, all but two of them having 3–6 members and important patrons. The remaining three minstrels whom he rewarded, encountered during Howard's travels, had no apparent patrons. His accounts for these few years also include many other payments to singers, trumpeters, waits, harpers, and fiddlers, not to mention hockers, taborers, heralds, players, Clerks of St Nicholas, and bearwards, for performances at Stoke-by-Nayland or elsewhere. The patrons of the minstrels whom he paid included the King (twice); the lords of Oxford, St John, Suffolk, and Warwick; Howard himself; and the village of Polstead.

Finally, during the fifteenth centuy, in 1470 the city of Ipswich ordered that if players or pipers performed at the council's dinners, they should be paid by a collection taken at the dinner (si lusores siue ffistyllatores veniu*eri*n*t* ad prandiu*m* q*uo*d tu*n*c stipend*ium* eo*rum* erit collect*um* ad prandiu*m*). And in 1496–97, the Jesus and Corpus Christi Guild in the village of Creeting St Mary paid one Hert and a taborer, both of whom it called minstrels (It*e*m payd to the menstrell*es* þ*a*t is to sey hert and the taborer xij d). Thereafter, every year between 1500 and 1538 the guild paid an unnamed minstrel and a banner bearer for what must have been the guild's procession.

The greater number of the minstrels in these fifteenth-century records had patrons; they were not mere wanderers. They must have been highly skilled performers, however we have almost no evidence of their repertoires. The one exception is a fifteenth-century manuscript song book, originally the property of an unnamed Ipswich minstrel. Written on paper in English and Latin, it has 63 leaves (including 10 preliminary pages) measuring 150mm x 110mm (text area average 115mm x 65mm). It bears the name of a later owner, William Roberts, 1574, on f 62v, and was purchased by the Bodleian Library in 1887. During the nineteenth century, it was repaired and bound in a hard cover. The book is a collection of song lyrics, some with parts, some in quatrains (aaaa, bbbb, etc.); several pages of musical notation; and one drawing or figure. Most of the songs are spiritual in nature.

The first half of the sixteenth century of course brought great social, political, and religious tumult to Suffolk, and, with it, changes to the musical landscape. In the three decades leading up to the dissolution of the monasteries, more performers and more kinds of performers, ironically, are recorded at the Abbey of Bury

St Edmunds than during the entire fourteenth century. Tradition continued at the Abbey in that it paid boy bishops in every surviving account between 1506 and 1537. During those years, the Abbey also paid a juggler, singers, a trumpeter, and a luter. However, most striking is the profusion and variety of professionals that come to the Abbey. In making payments, account rolls distinguish clearly between minstrels (musicians), lusores (actors), histriones (actors often associated with music), mimi (waits), and "ludentibus" (presumably local players), as when, for example, in 1531–32, officials made a single payment of 2s to "diu*ersis* lusorib*us* et histrionib*us*" who appear to have performed together. The patrons of all these professional performers were most often the king or the prince, and in other cases were court-connected members of the nobility. Another striking feature of the accounts is the tendency of troupes to cluster. In 1506–07, for example, the Abbey paid the minstrels of the King, the lord Prince, lord Arundel, and the Earl of Oxford. In 1529–30, the Abbey paid the players of the King, the Earl of Derby, and the Dukes of Norfolk and Somerset, which would be a great number of actors in any venue. Local records also contain reference to the tenement of a local minstrel, John Adams.

To the point of the article, in the Abbey records from the fifteenth through the early sixteenth centuries, the term "minstrel" recurs throughout the entire period of the records without any indication that it might also mean "actor" as well as musical performer. From 1506–07 through 1536–37, references to actors appear alongside minstrels in the accounts (as in payments to ludentes, lusores, histriones, and mimi). If anything, the dual appearances of minstrels and actors in account rolls strengthen the impression that minstrel meant only musical performer in early sixteenth-century Bury. The term "minstrel" does not appear after 1536 in Bury records, having been supplanted by the word "musician"; the records give no evidence linking minstrels with dramatic performance in Bury.

Through the centuries at Bury, all but one of the payments that were specifically dated within the year of the account (and many were not so dated) to minstrels and other entertainers occurred on feast days: St Edmund (9 times); St Nicholas and Easter (4 each); Christmas and The Ascension (2 each); and St John Baptist, St Edward, All Saints, Purification, Lent, and St Mark (1 each). Over the centuries, the records identify only two venues—the hall, and the camera of the Prior, where companies of actors and minstrels were paid in single entries each.

The same pattern (relative to minstrels) exists in the sixteenth-century records of Mettingham College, but with a much greater volume of evidence. The college paid musical entertainers every year between 1506–07 and 1525–26, when such payments forever cease. While it sometimes paid other kinds of entertainers (a luter, a lyrist, jugglers (twice), a taborer, and players (three times), the college paid minstrels every year between 1506 and 1526 (often several different minstrels in a year, often those performing in troupes, sometimes those performing with players or jugglers). In describing musical performers, the college seems never to have identified them as anything other than minstrels, always distinguishing them from other kinds of performers. However, the pattern in their patrons does differ from that at Bury. Identified patrons or places include the King (5 visits); the lords Jacob Hobart, Oxford, and Willoughby (1 each); the city of Norwich (2), and unnamed gentlemen (2); but by far the greatest number of payments (16) went to unnamed minstrels who had no apparent patron. It would seem that, unlike Bury, Mettingham did not become a gathering place for the great and the good and their troupes during its final days, though it certainly remained a reliable sponsor for minstrels and other performers.

The term "minstrel" continued its currency elsewhere in the county as well during the early sixteenth century, showing a bridge of continuity extending from the final quarter of the fifteenth century through the first quarter of the sixteenth century. Several small communities employed minstrels. In 1511, the Guild of St Peter in the village of Bardwell paid wages to three minstrels (Bardwell also had a parish "game" or play). In the village of Creeting St Mary, the Guild of Jesus and Mary did much the same. In 1468 (the year it was founded), the guild's records had listed two minstrels among its original members. Until its records cease in 1538, the Creeting guild includes annual payments to "the minstrel" in every year for which records survive. Creeting had something called a "sporting," and an elaborate procession to which the minstrel, a taborer, and a banner carrier contributed. At Stoke-by-Nayland, one Thomas Stowe, "the mynstrell of hadleyth [Hadleigh]," performed twice for the Howards in 1483 (two years earlier, "the plaiers of Hadley" had performed there). The wording of the entry appears to indicate that the minstrel Stowe was employed by the town of Hadleigh. Entries giving similar indications occur elsewhere, for example: the minstrels of Colchester, Essex, who performed before the Howards on 29 December 1482 (as had the Waits of Colchester much earlier, on 21 April 1467); "le menstrell of wa*n*gford," paid by Thetford Priory in 1524–25; and "Iohn Bannok otherwyse callid Barbour the mynstrell of Stradbrook," so identified by Bannok himself in his will in 1542. If all these minstrels were indeed employed by the towns with which they were identified, then they were skilled enough to be hired by a substantial village or a small town, and they would therefore have had duties resembling those of waits in larger places (ceremonial, customary, seasonal, religious).

Similarly during the late fifteenth century, the household accounts of John, Lord Howard of Stoke-by-Nayland, contain numerous payments between 1481 and 1483 to minstrels whose patrons were nobility (lords Gloucester and Buckingham, Lady Norfolk); or towns (Colchester, Hadleigh, and Harkstead);

or a gentleman (Mr. Woodes). Other of the minstrels whom he paid had no apparent patron, and received much smaller amounts. Several others whom the accounts refer to as "the minstrels," or as "James," or who mended the lutes, were apparently Norfolk's own household musicians. Other musical performers who were paid by Howard during these two years had many names (waits, singers, harpers, children of the chapel, trumpeters, schalmers, piper, taborers), but during these early Tudor years throughout Suffolk (as in the religious houses), "minstrel" appears to mean a musician of one kind or another, sufficiently skilled (in most cases) to attract a patron, and to earn a living by performing. Though minstrels might take part in dramatic productions, "minstrel" was never demonstrably another name for "actor" or another kind of performer. This pattern at Bury and Mettingham would seem to contradict the comment of Walter L. Woodfill, that "at the beginning of the sixteenth century 'minstrel' seems to have been used to designate all kinds of public entertainers, and more particularly those who acted and performed music."

By the end of 1525, the word "minstrel" had begun its long, gradual descent in the records, eventually giving way to "musician." However, in a few places it remained current for some time. The accounts from the Abbey at Bury St Edmunds (and a lease) from 1526–27 through 1536–37 reward minstrels (the lease mentions one), as opposed to the mimi, histriones, lusores, and a luter whom they also reward. Notably, the abbey paid the minstrels of the king four times during that decade. The above cited "menstrell of Wangford" was paid for a performance at Thetford Priory in 1524–25. The Jesus and Mary Guild of Creeting St Mary continued to pay "The Minstrel" annual wages for a variety of duties until 1538, when the guild's records end. In writing their wills, three Suffolk performers described themselves as minstrels: John Bannock alias Barber, "the minstrel of Stradbroke" in 1542; William Guyblon, minstrel, of Sudbury, in 1552; and (in his own will) Daniel Wade, minstrel, of Westleton as late as 1607.

Ipswich presents an interesting case in the evolution of the two terms. Early in the reign of Elizabeth I, city accounts and minute books used the two terms alternatingly in referring to the town's waits. The master of the waits was "the minstrel" in 1557–58, 1561–62, 1566–67, 1567–68, 1568–69, 1571–72, 1573–74, and 1575–76, but "the musician" in 1565–66, 1571–72, 1576–77, and 1580–81. When referring collectively to Martin and his company, the records alternate terms in the same way. The records also refer to two other musical performers who had run afoul of the law (in 1555 and 1573) as "minstrels." Early Elizabethan Ipswich used the two terms interchangeably.

After 1576, with two exceptions the term "minstrel" disappears almost entirely from the Ipswich records. The records do refer to "the blind ministrell" who received 16d in 1583–84; and to one "Iohn Iohnson mynstrell for taking paines in the m*ar*ket by the direcc*i*on of Mr Bailiff*es*," who received 20s (though whether for music or something else is not clear), but the city thereafter refers to its musical performers as musicians or waits only. The term "minstrel" also disappears concerning itinerant professionals. The records always describe the many troupes that visited Elizabethan Ipswich as "players," never as "minstrels." The impression arises that as a term of art, "minstrel" eroded in Ipswich, being increasingly used to indicate a person of lower performative or professional rank among musical entertainers. One wonders if the change had something to do with the near total monopoly (and change in status) that waits enjoyed in Elizabethan and Stuart towns.

The shift from "minstrel" to "musician" in the Suffolk records coincides with a complex historical moment, culturally speaking. The dissolution of the monasteries destroyed a major host to performers, who thereafter would have had to depend on towns and villages, the non-cloistered church, and private households more than they already had. As the sixteenth century neared its end, nearly all troupes of minstrels and actors sponsored by lords had disappeared from the Suffolk records. Only a few towns, the royal family, and a very few great noblemen continued to sponsor traveling performers. But paradoxically, as the number of patrons declined, musical performers, now identifying themselves as musicians, emerged from anonymity. It appears that the term bestowed entrepreneurial identity and a craftsman's level of skill, whereas "minstrel" often came with anonymity and a degree of servitude. The amount of detail about musicians, their instruments, and their position in society grew exponentially in wills, family papers, and civic records. Composers appeared. Whether or not this greater amount of evidence always reflects a general rise in the quality of musicianship is less than certain: in preparing the celebration of All Saints Day in 1638, the burgesses of Ipswich found it necessary to order the bailiffs to "p*ro*vide the best Musicke they Canne gett to playe Afore them."

The nobility and gentry had always had household musicians, of course, and some of those in Suffolk during the sixteenth and seventeenth centuries were notable indeed. The distinguished composer and madrigalist John Wilbye (1574–1638) served for many years as musician and musical tutor to the Kitsons at Hengrave Hall. The admired composer Edward Johnson (1572–1601) served the Kitsons in that same capacity. The musicians' chamber at Hengrave was lavishly equipped with musical instruments, related equipment, and music books. Musician and composer George Kirbye (d. 1634) "was employed as a domestic musician at Rushbrooke Hall near Bury St Edmunds, the seat of Sir Robert Jermyn. Rushbrooke Hall was but a few miles from Hengrave and it is thought that Kirbye "must have had personal contacts" with Wilbye. In 1600, the household accounts of the Adairs of Flixton Hall recorded rewards to the musicians "Stubbs" and "Connoway," who appear to have been the family's household musicians, especially since they also repaired the family's musical instrument as required.

The records do certainly leave the impression that musicians were developing an independent identity as professionals who aspired to be (or were) gentlemen. For example, William Firmage, musician and musical tutor, of Rougham near Bury (d. 1622), bequeathed

> to Mr Robert Drury of Rougham my Sett of English and Italian Madrigalles Manuscript to 3. 4. 5. and 6 voices, which haue my name on the Covers and are in Mr Kirby of Bury his Custody and to his wife Mrs Drury I giue my picture which is likewise in Mr Kirby his Custody, Item I giue to Mr Iohn Drury of Rougham my Sett of Latin Mottetes to 4.5. and 6. voices, and all other my Sett*es* of singing bookes both printed and Manuscript (except those hereafter bequeathed to Mr Kirby) togither with Mr Morlyes introduction Item I giue to Mr Henry Kirchefeild of little Saxham my base vyoll with the Case and all my bookes of vyoll lessons both printed and manuscript Item I giue to Mr George Kirby of Bury my sett*es* of bookes of ffancies and atin Mottetts to 5. and. 6. voices and also my Lattin Mottett*es* to 7. and 8. voices w*hi*ch remaine in his hand*es* yett vnfinished, together with all my dutch Roiall ruled paper.

At the same time, Firmage could also bequeath lands, houses, and tenements freehold, plus lands leased from the Lord of the Manor of Great Ashfield to his brother; £60 to his sister; £20 each to numerous nieces and nephews; and gold rings or other costly items to other relatives.

Among others identified as musicians who turn up in wills are John Roke, of Aldringham (d 1611); and William Allgate, widower, of Bury (d. 1642), who bequeathed a messuage (a dwelling with outbuildings and a yard or garden) and all its properties to his servant Agnes. Three men who may have been musicians, but are not identified as such in the records, left musical instruments to their children. John Pettaugh, a wealthy yeoman, of Framsden (d. 1620), left to his daughter Katherine "þe virginalls standinge in my haull." Barnabas Gibson, gentleman, of Haughley (d. 1634), bequeathed unto "Samuell my sonne my bigest silver Cup and my vyall." Marian Lyster, widow, of Alpheton (d. 1634) bequeathed "vnto Iohanna Cunisby my Yongest daughter the payre of virginalls that were her ffathers."

In early modern Suffolk, minstrels, fiddlers, and others identified by their instrument of choice gave way to musicians and waits sponsored mainly by towns, schools, households, and members of the royal family.

Musicians and Drama

There is ample indication that musical entertainers in Suffolk contributed to drama, custom, and ceremony, although the precise nature of those contributions is often murky because of vagueness in the records.

The earliest possible evidence occurs in payments made at Ipswich on 1 January 1296/97 to three minstrels named "Grisecote / Visage, & Magote Menestrall*is* facientib*us* eodem modo menstralcias," (performing [before the Lady Elizabeth] as had minstrels before them). While they are clearly identified as minstrels, their names sound like characters rather than given names, suggesting (to me) that their minstrelsy involved role-playing of some kind, perhaps farcical, before the royal bride-to-be. Also at this celebration, among a group of minstrels paid on the day of the nuptials, was "Thome le ffol," suggesting the likelihood of a performance incorporating music and mimetic comic activity.

One finds performances combining minstrelsy and play at religious houses as well. In 1405, Mettingham College paid a minstrel playing with a horse ("It*e*m dat*um* cuid*a*m menstrall' ludent' cu*m* equo iiij d"). It is hard to imagine this event as drama, but it certainly involved a play or dialogue of some sort between man and beast. But other events at Mettingham do seem to indicate legitimate dramatic performances together by players and minstrels. Among the many payments to visiting minstrels and players, on seven occasions the college paid minstrels and lusores (amateur local players) together as a single troupe, with a single amount, for a performance, usually one staged at Christmas, but at other times as well:

1469–70 It*e*m vij ministrall*is* & lusorib*us* in temp*o*re Nat*ale* d*omi*ni et cito post ij s.
1483–84 Et ij*bus* ministral*is* & j lusori viij d.
1486–87 Et diu*sersis* ministrall*is* & lusorib*us* temp*o*re Nata*le* D*omi*ni iiij s. iiij d.
1497–88 Et soluti & dat*um* lusorib*us* et menstrallis in temp*o*re nat*ale* d*omi*ni iij s. iiij d.
1508–09 Et dat*um* lusorib*us* & mi*ni*strall' in Nat*ale* D*omi*ni iiij s. viij d.
1518–19 Et diu*ersis* Ministrall*is* & lusorib*us* ad diu*ersis* vices xj s.
1522–23 Et dat*um* diu*ersis* ministrall*is* / et lusorib*us* in reward*o* viij s. viij d.

In nearly all of these entries (save 1518–19) it is clear that the local players and the minstrels were both contributing to a single production.

Minstrels visitng Mettingham College also appear to have been performing with other kinds of entertainers, although one cannot be certain that, in some cases, the scribes were not lumping several payments into a single sum:

1467–68 It*e*m duob*us* ministrall*is* & alij ho*min*i fingent*es* Stultu*m* viij d.
1470–71 It*em* quinq*ue* ministrall*is* & custodib*us* vrseor*um* duab*us* vicib*us* diu*er*sor*um* ij s. ix d.
1519–20 Et dat*um* ministrall*is* d*omi*ni Reg*is* /& eius Ioculator*is* xl d.
1520–21 Et dat*um* Ministrall' et s*er*vientib*us* gen*er*os*um* in Regard*o* x s.

1521–22 Et dat*um* s*er*vientib*us* magnator*um* / Ministrall' & alijs x s. iiij d.
1523–24 Et dat*um* Ioculator' & Ministrall' d*omi*ni Reg*is* vj s.

In 1443–44, the Prioress of Bungay Priory granted 4d to a minstrel—the wait of Bungay—for his tenement, at a play that was staged before her, apparently in the Christmas season (Et dat*i* cuid*a*m ministrallo ocup*anti* offici*um* de le wayte in Bungey ad vnu*m* interludu*m* cora*m* d*omi*na monstrat*um* *pro* tene*men*-*to* suo infra temp*us* Natal*e* d*omi*ni hoc A*nn*o iiij d). It is unclear whether his reward was recompense for a contribution to the play.

Ipswich provides rare evidence of waits performing not only as musicians but as actors. In 1568–69, the Council paid 10s to "Martin the mynstrell & his Companye for playing the ffooles in the halle" (Ipswich, Suffolk Record Office, C/3/3/2/9, f [10v]). The Ipswich waits clearly had dimension. On 11 April 1595, the Council approved the petition of John Bettes and Ralph Oldham, masters of the waits, allowing their "goinge beyonde the seas this summer next" (Ipswich, Suffolk Record Office, C/2/2/2/1, f 182v). The major annual performative civic events in Elizabethan Ipswich were activities attendant to The Guild Feast and to the celebration of the Queen's Coronation Day. Civic records (discussed above) confirm that both events might include drama, pageantry, speeches, and shows. The pattern of payments in the accounts also indicates that the waits customarily contributed to both events. In 1578, for example, civic accounts paid the waits for contributions to a Guild Feast that, in that year, certainly included pageants, given payments to both the pageant maker and the waits (for their music at the guild).

With the dismantling of the chantries and the establishment of local grammar schools under Edward VI, the role of schoolmasters in producing school drama grew exponentially in Suffolk, as it did everywhere. In 1608, the Governors of King Edward School awarded John Greene the Musician 10s "for his Musick at the Com*m*odye." They paid him the same amount in 1619/20.

In the villages and towns of Ipswich, given the example of Creeting St Mary (discussed above), which paid guild minstrels, drummer, and bearer of the banner, minstrels must have played a central part in customary processions—which had mimetic elements. Given the large plays produced in such places as Boxford and Bungay, and the contributions of minstrels in the large play texts for which Suffolk is famous, and the number of banns that were cried, minstrels must have made significant contributions to parish drama. But they have left few traces in parish records.

Summary

The records reveal literally hundreds of musical entertainers in Suffolk between 1296 and 1642 (the period covered by this study). The great number of those performers had patrons, mainly the nobility and gentry, towns and villages, and religious foundations, although a great many performers who have no declared patron at all appear as well. Among the nobility and gentry, the patrons included both men and women. They might sponsor individual performers or troupes, both of musicians and players. Because of their institutional nature, the records tend to show musical performers being paid in connection with important religious, civic, and seasonal dates, and in connection with other events on those days (ranging from feasts to processions to ceremonies to drama). Troupes of local players, on the other hand, who were advertising their own parish play, might sometimes turn up on dates close to the production of their play.

The records document a number of local musical performers doing local performances, of course, but authorities also paid vast numbers of itinerant minstrels and other musical entertainers. Those performers' itineraries, made with appreciation of local expectations, must have created a kind of regional repertoire. One wonders if local audiences demanded to hear old favorites, or welcomed "musical news," much as traveling players brought literal news and new plays. Few actual evidences of repertoires survive, but performance dates ranged from holy days (a great many) to guild days, from weddings to village processions to alehouse music, from masques to household music and dance.

A few blind minstrels turn up in the records, exclusively in, and under the care of, towns. So do boys, apprenticed to musicians, primarily waits. The records also reveal several instrument suppliers, instrument makers and repairers of instruments (though resident musicians usually handled that task for families), located in Bury, in Norwich, and in far-away London. Every known early musical instrument turns up in the records, from viols to virginals to pipes to fifes and drums. In the wills of the Suffolk gentry, it is more often the daughters than the sons to whom the father bequeaths musical instruments—often virginals; but in the wills of professional musicians, in Suffolk it is always the son(s) or other male relatives who receive the instruments and supplies.

The records show minstrels and musicians contributing to dramatic events, but not as copiously, or as unambiguously, as one would like. During the Elizabethan years, one sees a hierarchy evolving among musical performers. One also sees waits emerging as entrepreneurs with a license to augment their income by traveling to performances elsewhere. By virtue of their employment by the masters and burgesses, waits came to enjoy a near monopoly over musical performance in towns. The records show them operating as companies controlled by one master. The town hired the master; the master hired his company; the master and company appear to have had a veto in permitting other visiting musical entertainers to perform.

Most striking is the evolving role of patrons and sponsors, who changed with the times. In the medieval period, the city of Ipswich, the religious houses of Bury and Mettingham College, and the powerful local religious guilds served as major hosts. But with the dissolution of the monasteries, the dismantling of local guilds and chantries, and the near disappearance of the nobility as patrons, the most reliable patrons and hosts became towns as the sixteenth century neared its end. Itinerancy and sustained, reliable, playing circuits eroded and decayed away. The greatest enemy of the inherited musical culture became the increasingly vicious and inhibiting wars of ideology, religion, and politics.

Notes

1. London, The National Archives (hereafter TNA): PRO E 135/2/22, ff 1v col 1 and 2 col 2, 24, 29, 30–61v; and Cambridge, University Library, Add MS 6969, f 173v.
2. Ipswich, Suffolk Record Office (hereafter SRO), EE 1/I/2/1, ff 12, 13, 49v, 67, 83, 91v, 103v, 196, 224, 147, 168, 197v, 239, 257v; Ipswich, SRO, EE 1/I/2/2, ff 24v, 65v, 68, 88v, 116v, 128, 139B, 149, 160B, 183v, 220v.
3. Ipswich, SRO, EE 1/I/2/1, ff 12, 13, 49v, 50v, 52v, 67–7v, 77–7v, 80, 82v–3.
4. Ipswich, SRO, EE 1/I/2/1, ff 103v.
5. Ipswich, SRO, EE 1/I/2/1, ff 138v, 139–9v, 146v, 148, 158v, 165v, 194, 223, 235.
6. Civic records throughout England include payments to blind harpers, fiddlers, or musicians. Apparently, many local officials found it both charitable and practical to support the teaching of blind youths to sing and play. Shakespeare knew of them. In *Love's Labors Lost*, the chastened Berowne swears to Rosaline that he will never more "woo in rhyme, like a blind harper's song" (V.ii.405) (G. Blakemore Evans, ed., *The Riverside Shakespeare* [Boston: Houghton Mifflin, 1974] 206). Sir Philip Sidney, in his "Defense of Poesie," confesses that "I never heard the old song of Percy and Douglas [The Ballad of Chevy Chase] that I found not my heart moved more than with a trumpet; and yet it is sung by some blind crowder [a Welsh fiddle]" (M. H. Abrahms and Stephen Greenblatt, *The Norton Anthology of English Literature*, 7th ed., 2 vols [NY: Norton, 2000], 1:945).
7. Ipswich, SRO, EE 1/I/2/1, ff 180v, 182, 183, 211.
8. Ipswich, SRO, EE 1/I/2/1, ff 5, 12, 52v, 80v, 114–14v, 123v, 136v, 180, 195v, 224, 237v, 238v, 257, 259v, 274, 277v, 280, 316; Ipswich, SRO, EE 1/I/2/2, ff 127, 138v, 139v.
9. Ipswich, SRO, EE 1/I/2/1, ff 80v, 146v, 168.
10. Ipswich, SRO, HD 1538/156/13, mb 5; Ipswich, SRO, HD 1538/156/7, single membrane; Lowestoft, SRO, 116/E1/1, pp 18, 36, 52, 63, 68, 71; 116/E1/1, pp 2–3, 8, 12, 19, 27, 33–6, 40–43, 45–54, 153, 103, 109, 184.
11. Cambridge, Un\iversity Library, Add MS 6969, f 273; Bury, Suffolk Record Office, H2/3/4/11, f 54; H 1150/2, ff 48v, 38v, 44v, and 49.
12. Bury, SRO, H1150/2, ff 42v, 46v; E5/9/203.15 [item 3], mb 2; E5/9/203.16 [item 6], mb 2; E5/9/203.16 [item 5], mb 1; E5/9/203.16 [item 4], mb 1; E5/9/202.1, p 99; IC 500/1/99/68, single sheet; IC 500/1/101/84, sheets [1–2].

13. Ipswich, SRO, EE 6/1144/10, ff 101v–02, 121v, 172v, 204, 262, 275v.
14. Ipswich, SRO, FC 185/E1, ff 43, 85, 126, and 130.
15. Ipswich, SRO, FC 185/E1, ff 61, 67v, 71, 99, 124v, 128v, 114v, 121v.
16. For example, musicians of many kinds performed at the wedding of, and related celebrations for, Lady Elizabeth, daughter of Edward, at Ipswich in 1296 (London, BL (hereafter BL), Add MS 7965, mb 52). In 1470, the town ordered that any pipers or entertainers who might perform at the town's dinner should be paid by a collection taken at that dinner (Et Ordinacio concess*um* est q*uo*d si lusores siue ffistyllatores veniu*eri*nt ad prandiu*m* q*uo*d tu*n*c stipend*ium* eo*rum* erit collect*um* ad prandiu*m*) (London, BL, Add MS 30158, f 29). On 4 November 1538, the burgesses paid the minstrels of several great lords (Ipswich, Suffolk Record Office, C/3/3/1/3, mb [8].
17. Nathaniell Bacon, *The Annalls of Ipswche* (1654), edited by William H. Richardson (Ipswich, 1884) 212.
18. Ipswich, SRO, C/3/3/2/5, f [4v] (1561–2); C/3/4/1/5, ff [3v] and [5] (1565–66); Nathaniell Bacon, *The Annalls of Ipswche* (1654), edited by William H. Richardson (Ipswich, 1884), 271 (1566); C/2/10/3/12, f [4v]; C/3/2/1/1, f 166; and C/3/4/1/6, f [4] (1565–66).
19. Nathaniell Bacon, *The Annalls of Ipswche* (1654), edited by William H. Richardson (Ipswich, 1884) 278, and C/3/2/1/1, f 21v.
20. Ipswich, SRO, C/3/3/2/9, f [9v].
21. Ipswich, SRO, C/3/3/2/9, f [10v]; and C/3/3/2/12, f [4].
22. Ipswich, SRO, C/3/2/1/1, ff 50v, 102; C/3/4/1/9, ff [3v–4]. For other payments to William Martin for his music at the guild between 1572 and 1582, see C/3/4/1/7, f [4v]; C/3/4/1/8, f [11v]; and C/3/2/1/1, ff 120v, 135v, 171, 185, 213, and 223.
23. Ipswich, SRO, C/2/2/2/2/1, f 74v.
24. Nathaniell Bacon, *The Annalls of Ipswche* (1654), edited by William H. Richardson (Ipswich, 1884) 336.
25. Ipswich, SRO, C/3/4/1/17/1, f [4d]; C/3/4/1/17/2, f [3]; C/3/3/2/23, f 4v; and C/4/3/1/2, f 84.
26. Ipswich, SRO, EE 1/I/2/1, f 148.
27. Ipswich, SRO, C/2/2/2/1, f 121v.
28. Ipswich, SRO, C/2/2/2/1, f 122.
29. Ipswich, SRO, C/3/3/2/26, f [4].
30. Ipswich, SRO, C/2/2/2/1, f 150.
31. Ipswich, SRO, C/3/3/2/30, f [5]; C/3/2/1/2, ff 9v, 50.
32. Ipswich, SRO, C/3/3/2/6, f [6]; C/3/4/1/3, f [8v]; C/3/2/1/1, f 136; C/4/3/1/2, f [11v].
33. Ipswich, SRO, C/4/3/1/2, ff 14v–15; C/3/3/2/17, f [6v]; C/3/3/2/1, ff 171. See also ff 213, 185, 223.
34. Ipswich, SRO, C/3/2/1/1, f 83.
35. Ipswich, SRO, C/3/2/1/1, f 237v–8.
36. Ipswich, SRO, C/2/2/2/1, ff 89.
37. Ipswich, SRO, (C/3/4/1/17/1, f [5]); C/2/2/2/1, f 96; C/3/2/1/1, f 238; C/3/3/2/21, f [6].
38. Ipswich, SRO, C/3/3/2/25, f 122.
39. Ipswich, SRO, C/3/3/2/26, ff [7v–8]; C/4/3/1/3, ff 5, 54v.
40. Ipswich, SRO, C/3/3/2/28, f [6]; C/3/3/2/29, f [5v]; C/2/2/2/1, f 187; C/3/3/2/32, p 6.
41. Ipswich, SRO, C/3/4/1/27, f [4].
42. Ipswich, SRO, C/3/3/2/45, f [4]; C/3/2/1/2, ff 377v–78; and 409; C/3/3/2/61, f [4v]; C/3/2/1/2, ff 395; 409.
43. Ipswich, SRO, C/4/3/1/3, ff 143v, 216.
44. Ipswich, SRO, IC/AA1/72/56, single sheet; will of John Betts, Musician.

45. Ipswich, SRO, C/4/3/1/3, f 226.
46. Ipswich, SRO, C/3/2/1/2, f 162; C/4/3/1/4, f 19v.
47. Ipswich, SRO, C/3/2/1/2, ff 170, 179v; C/4/3/1/4, f 59v; C/3/2/1/2, f 196v; C/4/3/1/4 f 114v.
48. Ipswich, SRO, IC/AA1/98/36, single sheet; C/4/3/1/4, ff 120v–21.
49. Ipswich, SRO, C/3/3/2/45, ff [4–4v]; C/4/3/1/4, f 212; C/3/2/1/2, f 248.
50. London, BL, Cotton Appx.xxi, ff 130, 135v.
51. London, BL, Add MS 7965, f 52.
52. London, TNA: PRO C/66/140, mb 12 (Creeting); PRO, C/66/156, mb 24 (Roger of Bury); PRO, C/66/191, mb 1 (Manpryne of Bury); PRO, C/66/141, mb 4d (William of Bury); PRO, E 36/278, f 43 (war horse at Bury).
53. London, BL, Royal MS 6 B X, ff 141–41v; for a list of most surviving officials' accounts, see Rodney M. Thomson, *The Archives of the Abbey of Bury St Edmunds*, Suffolk Record Society 21 (Woodbridge: Boydell and Brewer, 1980), 69–70. This fragment is not included in that list.
54. London, BL, Add MS 40,069, ff 36, 42v, 52v, 58, 67v (Mettingham); Bury, SRO, A/6/1/16.4, mb 2d (Bury); Ipswich, SRO, HD 1538/271/6, single mb (Ipswich Priory).
55. Innumerable pages in London, BL: Add MSS 40069, 33985, 33986, 33987, 33988, 33989; Chicago, University of Chicago Library 946, f [1v] (Mettingham) (all specific entries for Mettingham will be included in *REED: Suffolk*, forthcoming); Ipswich, SRO, HD 1538/156/13, mb 5 (Bungay Priory); London, TNA: PRO SC 6/HENVII/691, mb 3 (Felixstowe).
56. The remaining noble patrons whose minstrels performed at Mettingham are: Bishop Eliens, Duke of Exeter, Lord Thomas Marney, Duchess of York (3 times each); Count Westmoreland, Lord Bowcer (or Bonnser), Duchess of Norfolk, Essex, Lord of Oxford, Lord Grey (Count Caucie or Kantie) (2 times each); an unnamed bishop, Northumberland, Lord John, Clarence, Count de March, Bishop of Winchester,Walsingham, Count Marishiall (Marshall), Sir Thomas Erpingham, Lord de Stales, Lord John Bone, Duke of York Arundell, Lord Jacob Hobart (knight) (1 time each).
57. For example, between 1403–4 and 1406–7 (London, BL: Add MS 33985, ff 16, 23, 29, 35); between 1450–51 and 1453–4 (London, BL: Add MS 33986, ff. 35, 60v, 78v); and many other instances in the registers.
58. London, BL: Add MS 33987, f 103.
59. London, BL: Add MS 33985, ff 113, 125, 130; Add MS 33987, ff 45, 55; Add MS 33988, f 76; Add MS 33989, f 92; Add MS 33988, ff 69v, 87v; Add MS 33989, ff 9, 19.
60. Bury, SRO, A/6/1/4, mb 2, A/6/1/5, mb 2d; Ipswich, SRO, HD 1538/88/25, mb 2d; Bury, SRO, A/6/1/6, mb 2d; Ipswich, SRO, HD 1538/88/19, mb 2d; London, TNA: PRO SC 6/HENVII/1692, single mb.
61. London, BL: Add Roll 16556, mb 21 (Mowbray); Ipswich, SRO, HA 411/5/2/1/1, mbs 3, 4 (de la Pole); London, TNA: PRO C 47/4/8B, ff 8v–10, 13, 14, 17, 23v (De Bryene).
62. London, BL, Add MS 46349, ff 49, 20, 65–5v, 69v, 74v, 83, 92; and Beriah Botfield, "*Accounts and Memoranda of Sir John Howard, first Duke of Norfolk, A.D. 1462, to A.D. 1471*," in *Manners and Household Expenses of England in The Thirteenth and Fifteenth Centuries, Illustrated by Original Records* (London, 1841).
63. London, BL, Add MS 30158, f 29; London (Ipswich), TNA: PRO E 135/2/22, f 24 (Creeting).
64. Oxford, Boldeian Library, MS Eng. Poet.e.1. See also a microfilm copy (reference J479) of the original manuscript book at SRO, Ipswich.
65. For all the performers paid by the abbey in Bury between 1506–07 and 1536–37, see: London, TNA: PRO SC 6/HENVII/1693, single mb (1506–07); London, TNA: PRO

SC 6/3481/70, mb 3 (1515); Bury, SRO, A/6/1/17, single mb dorse (1520–21); London, TNA: PRO SC 6/3396, mb 5 (1524–25) and SC 6/HENVIII/3397, single mb and dorse (1524–25); London, BL: Add Roll 53140, mbs 4v–5 (1527–28); London, TNA: PRO SC 6/HENVIII/3394, single mb dorse (1529–30), SC 6/HENVIII/3395, single mb (1530–31), SC 6/HENVIII/3391, single mb (1531–32), SC 6/HENVIII/3392, mb 3 (1531–32), and SC 6/HENVIII/3398, mb 2d (1536–37); and Ipswich, SRO, HD 1538/88/29, mb 4d (1536–37).

66. London, TNA: PRO SC 6/HENVIII/3392, mb 3 (1531–32); London, TNA, PRO SC 6/HENVII/1693, single mb (1506–07); London, TNA: PRO SC 6/HENVIII/3394, single mb dorse (1529–30).
67. Bury, SRO, A/6/2/1, p 43.
68. Innumerable pages in London, BL: Add MSS 33989, 33990, 40070; (all specific entries for Mettingham will be included in *REED: Suffolk*, forthcoming).
69. Bury, SRO, FL 522/11/20, pp 4, 6 (Bardwell); Cambridge, Cambridge University Library: Add MS 6969, f 72 (Bardwell); and London, TNA: PRO E 135/2/22, ff 1v col 1, 24, 29–61v intermittent, 3, 4–5v, 7, 8, 11, 14, 15v (Creeting St Mary).
70. London, Society of Antiqruries, MS 77, ff 33v, 43; MS 76, f 106.
71. London, Society of Antiquaries, MS 77, ff 31v; London, BL, Add MS 46349, f 138 (Stoke); Cambridge, Cambridge University Library, Add MS 6969, f 173v (Thetford Priory); Ipswich, SRO, IC/AA1/1/12/251, single sheet (Wangford).
72. London, Society of Antiquaries, MS 76, ff 60, 92, 94v; MS 77, ff 31v, 43, 33v.
73. London, Society of Antiquaries, MS 76, f 104; MS 77, f 105v.
74. London, Society of Antiquaries: MS 76, ff 136, 150; MS 77, f 104; MS 77, ff 32, and 130 (account of Howard's successor, Thomas Mowbray, Duke of York).
75. London, Society of Antiquaries, MS 76, ff 81, 90v, 96, 97, 102, 103, 108, 111v, 116, 117–17v, et pas.
76. Walter L. Woodfill, *Musicians in English Society from Elizabeth to Charles I* (Princeton: Princeton University Press, 1953) 57.
77. See: Bury, SRO, A/6/2/1, p 43 (1526–7); London, BL, Add Roll 53140, mb 5 (1527–8); London, TNA: PRO SC 6/HENVIII/3394, single mb d (1529–30); PRO SC 6/HENVIII/3395, single mb (1530–01); Ipswich, SRO, HD 1538/88/29, md 4d (1536–37); London, TNA: PRO SC 6/HENVIII/3398, mb 2d (1536–37).
78. Cambridge, Cambridge University Library, Add MS 6969, f 173 (Wangford); London, TNA: PRO E 135/2/22, ff 1v col 1, 24, 29–61v intermittent, 3, 4–5v, 7, 8, 11, 14, 15v (Creeting St Mary); Ipswich, SRO, IC/AA1/1/1/12/ 251, single sheet (Stradbroke); Bury, SRO, IC 500/1/12/49, single sheet (Sudbury); and Ipswich, SRO, IC/AA1/42/127, single sheet (Westleton).
79. For example, see Ipswich, SRO, C/3/2/1/1, f [6] (1557–58); C/3/3/2/5, f [4v] (1561–62); Nathaniel Bacon, *The Annalls of Ipswche* (Ipswich, 1884) 271 (1565); Ipswich, SRO, C/3/4/1/6, f [4] (1567–68); and Ipswich, SRO, C/3/3/2/9, f [9v] (1568–69).
80. Ipswich, SRO, C/3/3/2/21, f [4v], and C/3/2/1/2, f 21.
81. Ipswich, SRO, C/4/3/1/5, f 150.
82. David Brown, *The New Grove Dictionary of Music and Musicians*, edited by Stanley Sadie (London, 1980) 410–12 (Wilbye), 676 (Johnson), and 72 (Kirbye); Bury, SRO, IC 500/1/90/142, f [1] (Kirbye); Lowestoft, SRO, 741/HA 12/add 49, ff 7v–8 (Adair).
83. London, TNA: PRO B 11/139, ff 367–8 (Firmage). Firmage was a close friend of George Kirbye, the musician, of Bury St Edmunds. The Drurys and Gaudys were important members of the gentry in Suffolk.
84. Ipswich, SRO, IC/AA1/47/90, single sheet (Roke); and Bury, SRO, IC 500/1/99/68, single sheet (Allgate).

85. Ipswich, SRO, 1C/AA2/53, ff 11–13 (Pettaugh); Bury, SRO, IC 500/1/91 (15), sheets [9–10] (Gibson); Bury, SRO, IC 500/1/90 (175), single sheet (Lyster).
86. London, BL, Add MS 7965, f 52.
87. London, BL, Add MS 33985, f 23.
88. London, BL, Add MS 33987, f 114; Add MS 33988, ff 34v, 76; Add MS 33989, f 87v; Add MS 33990, f 76; Add MS 33989, ff 147v, 166v.
89. London, BL, Add MS 33987, ff 97v, 116v; 33989, ff 149v, 159v, 164v, 169.
90. Ipswich, SRO, HD 1538/156/13, mb 5.
91. Ipswich, SRO, C/3/3/2/9, f [10v]), C/2/2/2/1, f 182v, and C/3/2/1/1, ff 135v–136.
92. Bury, SRO, E5/9/203.16 [item 5, mb 1; Bury, SRO, H 1150/2, f 42v.

Residual Allegory in Elizabethan Drama: The One–Scene Psychomachia and Arresting the Vice

Alan C. Dessen

> [I]t is never safe to conclude...that allegory had died and no one knew where it was buried.
>
> —Rosemond Tuve[1]

The role of allegory in the plays of Shakespeare and his contemporaries has not been a hot (or even welcome) topic, particularly in an age when psychological realism remains the default position for readers, teachers, and theatrical professionals. However, two recent essays have challenged widely held views about the role of onstage allegory in sixteenth-century England, so that the topic has been given fresh life.

First, Vladimir Brljak argues that the firm belief that the Middle Ages was *the* Age of Allegory—that this alternative to Realism did not persist into the Renaissance—was a myth, "long overdue to join the Flat Earth, the Chastity Belt, the Angels Dancing on the Head of a Pin," and other exploded beliefs about that period. He demonstrates in detail how this "quarantine" of allegory emerged from the influential work of Jacob Burckhardt and later writers, especially John Addington Symonds. Burckhardt's distaste for allegory was so strong that his ultimate solution was "to approach an allegorical Renaissance painting as the work of two rather than a single author": first "the painter, who produces the material object of aesthetic appreciation which is the sole concern of the modern viewer," to be separated from "the patron peering over his shoulder," who commissioned the painting, "including its invisible, hence irrelevant, allegorical meaning." For Burckhardt, "any presence of allegory in the Renaissance" in the visual arts or literature was "to be explained as a residuum of the Middle Ages rather than a genuine aspect of the period." Symonds pointed to Udall's *Ralph Roister Doister* as the moment when English playwrights "emerge from medieval grotesquery and allegory into the clear light of actual life, into an agreeable atmosphere of urbanity and natural delineation." Brljak calls attention to "increasingly elaborate versions of the same story of how the drama liberated itself from allegorical personifications,"[2] a narrative that Willard Thorp sums up as "The Triumph of Realism."[3]

Second, Catherine Belsey in her essay on "transition" observes: "Part of the reason for the relative neglect of the moral plays...must be that they do not gratify our continued preference for realism. Allegory remains alien" whereas "mimetic assumptions go deep and can catch us unawares." She argues "that a recovered awareness of dramatic continuity can help to dispel such assumptions" and "can sharpen our sense of what is distinctive in Jonson, Shakespeare, and their contemporaries." These playwrights "altered the possibilities for English—and then world—drama, but they did so in the light of what had gone before, as well as in defiance of it. The early modern theater, in other words, both maintains and modifies the conventions of the past." As she notes, many new elements in the late sixteenth century broadened the range of drama (Seneca, Roman comedy, narrative romance, iambic pentameter), but "the process was cumulative, rather than evolutionary." If new developments altered the drama, "old habits could be incorporated or updated," so that they were not lost to sight. Linking old and new examples (e.g., *Horestes* and *Hamlet*) she notes that "Allegory was evidently not perceived as a constraint"; rather, "it allowed the presentation with a certain clarity of the issues that would confront later revengers."

As she sums up the situation: "In some respects, the new kinds self-evidently left the moral plays behind—but they were not forgotten." The changes may be decisive, but "at the same time, both generic and formal continuities are there to be traced." In her formulation: "The London theater neither emerged out of nowhere nor entirely repudiated its own past: instead, the professional dramatists whose works are still in our modern repertoire expanded and transformed a tradition that, since the mid-sixteenth century, had found successive ways to exceed the limits of homiletic drama, by incorporating new genres and modes of address."[4]

Like Belsey, I believe in continuity between allegory in the moral interludes and what follows in the 1580s and early 1590s. As a theatre historian my interest has been in the various means available to later playwrights—what I term the original *theatrical vocabulary*[5]—in this instance, ways of presenting ideas, abstractions, and key choices onstage. I do *not* have in mind soliloquies or other set speeches that clearly enunciate a Big Idea, devices that are readily recognizable to today's reader. Rather, my focus has been on other less visible techniques that can enhance the presentation of significant motifs or images. Outside of a few notable exceptions (the two angels in *Doctor Faustus*, Revenge in *The Spanish Tragedy*, Rumor in *2 Henry IV*, Time in *The Winter's Tale*) identifiable allegorical personae do not survive as part of the mainstream of Elizabethan professional drama. Moreover, as noted by Brljak and Belsey, a major component of today's prevailing logic of interpretation is a distaste for allegorical and didactic effects in drama, especially in Shakespeare's plays, for the triumph of realism narrative and its various successors—psychological and otherwise—have won the battle for the hearts and minds of Shakespeareans. Nonetheless, my thesis is that in the 1590s and thereafter a post-allegorical mode of presentation—what may be termed "residual" allegory (to borrow a distinction from Raymond Williams)[6]—*does* persist, albeit in adapted form. And thereby hangs my tale.

The Onstage One Scene Psychomachia

In what follows I will not invoke the allegorical personae scattered throughout lesser known plays. Rather, I will concentrate on two devices prevalent in the 1560s and 1570s that could be incorporated into the plays that follow. To start with a familiar moment, for his first appearance in *The Merchant of Venice* Launcelot Gobbo is given a comic turn of roughly thirty lines in which he debates whether or not to run away from his master, Shylock. The clown presents the arguments of two opposing forces, Conscience and the Devil, giving each side its own voice (and perhaps gestures) and likely placing himself in the middle as the chooser. Much of the fun arises from Launcelot's varying postures and inflections as he voices the strictures of Conscience and the insinuations of the Devil, perhaps only turning his head in turn for each speaker or, at the other extreme, leaping back and forth when he reaches "Bouge" versus "Bouge not." At the climax the clown sums up the two positions:

> "Conscience," say I, "you counsel well." "Fiend," say I, "you counsel well." To be rul'd by my conscience, I should stay with the Jew my master, who (God bless the mark) is a kind of devil; and to run away from the Jew, I should be rul'd by the fiend, who, saving your reverence, is the devil himself. Certainly, the Jew is the very devil incarnation, and in my conscience, my conscience is but a kind of hard conscience, to offer to counsel me to stay with the Jew. The fiend gives the more friendly counsel: I will run, fiend; my heels are at your commandement, I will run. (2.2.21–32)[7]

Here Launcelot's debate between the two voices or to-be-imagined entities is cast in a form still familiar to playgoers in the mid-1590s, a form associated with the moral drama and still visible occasionally at the end of the sixteenth century, most notably in the Good and Evil Angels that flank Doctor Faustus.

To characterize this technique, scholars who have dealt with the fifteenth- and sixteenth-century English moral plays have used the term *psychomachia* (war for the soul), derived from the title and focus of Prudentius's allegorical Latin poem, and have called attention to one of its major assets in drama or other narratives—the ability to break down X into component parts. One of the earliest scholars to write at length about the moral drama notes that in the early fifteenth-century *The Castle of Perseverance* "the subjective forces that in reality belong to man himself in the most personal sense were transformed by the poet into visible, external forces" so that, in effect, "the motives and impulses of man's own heart were taken from him, and, clothed in flesh and blood, given him again for companions."[8]

Unlike the soliloquy or aside, this approach to the onstage display of the workings of the mind is not compatible with the expectations of today's readers and playgoers.[9] A strong defense is provided by Wilbur Sanders in his discussion of the Good and Evil Angels in *Doctor Faustus* where he argues that such a technique is not "clumsily primitive" but rather "an immensely dramatic procedure." As he describes a representative scene: "The first effect of the interruption is to arrest all action on the stage, and to focus attention on the protagonist, suspended in the act of choice. Not until he speaks do we know to which voice he has been attending. It is the act of choice in slow motion, a dramatisation of his strained attention to the faint voices of unconscious judgment."[10] To readers today this effect may seem a blemish, but in the theatre such a slowing down of the process of choice can serve as a meaningful equivalent to a soliloquy or to a novelist's presentation of interior states of consciousness, especially for an audience attuned to such a technique.

In the earlier and more familiar moral dramas, this breaking down of the entity Humanum Genus, Everyman, or Mankind served as a strategy to organize an entire play. When the later moral dramatists turned to other strategies or paradigms, they still found use for such a device to break down X (an individual, a key choice, a kingdom) into its component parts that in turn could be represented onstage, often in a single scene. A revealing example is found in R. B.'s *Apius and Virginia* (1564)[11] where, after Apius agrees to the Vice's plan that will wrest Virginia from her family, the stage direction reads: "*Here let him make as though he went out and let Conscience and Justice come out of him, and let Conscience hold in his hand a lamp burning and let Justice have a sword and hold it before Apius' breast*" (500). Although Conscience and Justice have no lines while Apius is onstage, the judge himself supplies their half of the argument:

> But out I am wounded, how am I divided?
> Two states of my life, from me are now glided,
> For Conscience he pricketh me contemned,
> And Justice saith, judgment would have me condemned:
> Conscience saith cruelty sure will detest me:

And Justice saith, death in the end will molest me,
And both in one sudden me thinks they do cry,
That fire eternal, my soul shall destroy. (501–8)

Haphazard the Vice, however, mocks Conscience and Justice ("these are but thoughts" 510) and argues instead: "Then care not for Conscience the worth of a fable, / Justice is no man, nor nought to do able" (521–22). After Apius agrees to forgo his scruples ("let Conscience grope, and judgment crave"), Conscience and Justice are left alone onstage to lament his decision in psychological terms, as when Conscience complains: "I spotted am by willful will, / By lawless love and lust / By dreadful danger of the life. / By faith that is unjust" (538–41).

To act out the central decision in his play, R. B. has not resorted to a soliloquy or even to straightforward temptation by the Vice but has chosen to break down Apius's choice into its component parts. Somehow, at the moment when the judge is leaving the stage under the influence of the Vice and his own lust, Conscience and Justice are to "come out of" Apius (or "glide" from him, according to the dialogue), whether from behind his cloak or through some stage device. The theatrically emphatic presence of these two figures (with their striking entrance, their emblems, and their gestures) is then linked verbally to Apius's own conscience and sense of justice. Apius's subsequent exit with the Vice acts out his choice and spells out how he has abandoned his conscience and sense of justice in favor of his lust. Both the stage direction that indicates that Conscience and Justice are to "come out of" Apius and the Vice's insistence that "these are but thoughts" underscore how the inner workings of the protagonist's mind have been made external in a fashion particularly suited to onstage presentation.

The late moral dramatists regularly used such onstage psychomachias to display at length pivotal decisions, whether the choice of Knowledge of Sin over Infidelity (Lewis Wager, *The Life and Repentance of Mary Magdalene*, 1558), the choice of Covetous over Enough (William Wager, *Enough is as Good as a Feast*, 1560), or the choice of Faith over Despair (George Wapull, *The Tide Tarrieth No Man*, 1576). The technique survives in the 1590s, as witnessed by the Good and Evil Angels of *Doctor Faustus*, one or more angels who flank a despairing figure in Lodge and Greene's *A Looking Glass for London and England* (1590), and Launcelot's debate between Conscience and the Devil. In *A Warning for Fair Women* (1599), a pivotal event, the seduction of Mistress Sanders, is presented not through dialogue among the characters but by means of a dumb show that pits Lust versus Chastity. Like R. B., Wapull, and both Lewis and William Wager (or Marlowe with his two angels), this dramatist felt that such a visible orchestration of component parts was a workable method of putting the mind of a chooser on theatrical display at an important moment.

I invoke such choices to suggest some of the expertise in the late moral drama that regularly goes unrecognized and to call attention to comparable signifiers in the theatrical vocabulary in the 1580s and thereafter. My purpose is not to mount an assault upon all modern interpretation of Shakespeare's characters but rather to expand the options available to the reader or theatrical professional. When reading Shakespeare's plays we give privileged status to those features that do make sense in our terms, even when they are obvious non- or pre-realistic conventions like the soliloquy, but inevitably we play down or screen out other devices that do not conform to our horizon of expectations. Admittedly, Shakespeare and his contemporary playwrights seldom incorporate into their plays anything as obvious as Conscience and Justice who come out of Apius or Chastity and Lust who flank Mistress Sanders. Still, the principle of breaking down an entity or a decision into component parts for fuller display in the theatre was certainly not unknown to Shakespeare, as witnessed by Launcelot Gobbo's comic debate.

A Psychomachia Interlude

Relevant here is a workshop staging of a series of scenes at the University of Toronto in 2010 that involved a director (Peter Cockett), eleven actors, a costumer, and a dramaturge. Given the limited time and resources available, the director and I chose to focus on psychomachia tug-of-war scenes, both allegorical and post-allegorical, so that, after an initial segment from the Digby *Mary Magdalene*, an audience saw scenes from two late moral plays (the Despair sequence from Wapull's *The Tide Tarrieth No Man* and the appearance of Conscience and Justice in *Apius and Virginia*) followed by related tug-of-war scenes from Heywood's *1 The Iron Age*, the A-text *Doctor Faustus*, *Arden of Faversham*, *Antony and Cleopatra*, Dekker's *The Shoemakers' Holiday*, and *Cymbeline*. Between presentations the director provided a narrative bridge that offered plot summary and context, and, after the initial Digby scene, he offered a demonstration of the techniques that had been adopted.

At the outset Cockett noted "that we know virtually nothing about how early modern actors performed on stage." Rather, he declared the goal of this workshop was "to develop a visual rhetoric that can communicate moral arguments to an audience in a lively manner whether in a scene of overt moral allegory or a scene of apparent secular realism." Among the elements in this vocabulary were several rhetorical gestures: heaven "is upward, forward and to the performer's right"; hell is "downward, behind and to the performer's left." Other signifying actions included the right hand representing good, the left evil, and a left hand behind the body represented deceit. Virtues tend to be balanced and upright, whereas vice twists the body and puts it off-balance, so that in a configuration that the director termed "the penitent sinner" (e.g., Faustus with the Old Man) the actor played an in-between, indecisive state by reaching up to Heaven with his right hand while at the same time twisting down to the left. The goal was to suggest an alternative way to understand the character's struggles, an alternative that invites a different approach to performance than the modern method—"an allegorical style" that is recognizably not Realism. As the director summed up the situation: "Ultimately, all we can really say about our allegorical style is that it was developed with reference to period sources available to us and that it is recognizably not twenty-first-century realism."

Figure 1. Banishing Despair from Wapull's *The Tide Tarrieth No Man* (Toronto 2010).

What did this test reveal? No one involved in this project claimed that what emerged was a faithful reconstruction of the original staging. Nonetheless, the results of this workshop approach were enlightening. Most rewarding for me as an observer were the segments from the two moral plays, for here the staging revealed the assets of such visual rhetoric for making interior moral-psychological forces visible. The segment from *The Tide Tarrieth No Man* started with Faithful Few, a nun in white carrying a Bible, who forcefully delivered a speech on the power of Greed and Usury and the absence of Love that was followed by the appearance of Wastefulness "*poorly*" to lament "how wastefully have I, with Wantonness my wife, / Consumed our goods, substance and treasure" (1660, 1665–66). This despairing figure decides to "seek some place where I may, / Finish my life with Cord, or with knife" and is directed to "*feign a going out*" but is prevented by Faithful Few who "*plucketh him again*" (1691–93). This Virtue figure (the play's primary moral spokesman) called attention to God's mercy and got the despairing figure to kneel in prayer.

What pushed the scene to another level was the visible and audible presence of Despair. With Faithful Few looking on from stage right, Wastefulness (anticipating Marlowe's Faustus) asks "which way shall I run?" adding:

> I know it is folly unto God to call:
> For God I know my petition will shun,
> And into perdition I am now like to fall.
> Despair, despair. (1677–81)

At this point the stage direction reads: "*Despair enter in some ugly shape, and stand behind him*" to deliver a six-line speech (1684–89) that argues "to end thy life it is best" and "calling for mercy, is all but in vain." Despair was portrayed as a shabby black-hooded figure with ropes coiled around his neck and a pained (despairing) visage who hovered behind his victim. When Faithful Few started the counter argument, Despair initially knelt stage left of the two figures, then, with some tortured moans, gradually moved upstage, so that at the final word of the prayer ("banish hence / That wicked Monster of *Despair*") "*Despair flieth, and they arise*" (1709). This well acted moral exemplum of a preacher saving a wayward sinner would have made verisimilar sense without the presence of an allegorical entity, but this approach, given the actor's chilling depiction of Despair, took the effect to another level so as to demonstrate the potential assets of such a technique—a fine example of inner forces made visible in the allegorical mode. Such an onstage tug-of-war spells out the coordinates involved in a pivotal choice and makes external the moral geography of Despair and Faith in the chooser's mind.[12]

The same was true for the scene from *Apius and Virginia* where, as noted earlier, after Apius agreed to the Vice Haphazard's plan that will wrest Virginia from her family, the stage direction reads: "*Here let him make as though he went out and let Conscience and Justice come out of him.*" This surprising emergence was handled effectively by having the exiting Apius move upstage to the central curtained opening from which point the two figures emerged through the slits in his long black cloak. Meanwhile, Haphazard, who to this point had circled and dominated his victim, retreated downstage stage left to mock Conscience and Justice ("why these are but thoughts man") so that at Apius's exit all they could do was back off slightly and lower their heads as if in sadness.

Clearly, to act out the central decision in his play the playwright has chosen to break down Apius's choice into its component parts. The staging of the scene, however, reinforced this effect in ways I had not anticipated. In particular, the Vice's speeches as befits his name are full of references to "hap" and "hazard," and the actor supplied hand gestures to reinforce these usages. As this figure wove his spell over his victim, moreover, Apius too could be seen using the same gestures. His exit speech, with Conscience and Justice silently standing by, is peppered with *hap* and *haphazard*:

> And sayest thou so my sured friend, then *hap* as *hap* shall hit,
> Let Conscience grope, and judgment crave, I will not shrink one whit.
> I will persever in my thought, I will deflower her youth,
> I will not sure reverted be, my heart shall have no ruth,
> Come on proceed and wait on me, I will *hap* woe or wealth,
> *Hap* blunt, *hap* sharp, *hap* life, *hap* death, though *Haphazard* be of health
> (525–29, emphasis mine)

The last line, along with accompanying gestures, drove home a sense of the infection or pollution of this judge by the Vice and what he/it represents, so that, when combined with the two figures who "*come out of*" Apius and the Vice's insistence "why these are but thoughts," the inner workings of the protagonist's mind have been made external in a fashion particularly suited to onstage presentation.

Of the subsequent segments the most telling for me was Shakespeare's pre-Actium scene where for most of the time Antony was positioned stage left close to Cleopatra with Enobarbus, Canidius, and the soldier stage right. Clearly, the arguments from the three Romans to fight on land and to ignore Octavius's dare were outweighed not by Cleopatra's few lines on the subject ("By sea, what else?"; "I have sixty sails, Caesar none better" 3.7.28, 49) but by her very presence, as spelled out by Enobarbus before Antony's entrance: "Your presence needs must puzzle Antony, / Take from his heart, take from his brain, from's time / What should not then be spar'd" (10–12). I had suggested this scene because the tug-of-war had been obvious to me as a reader, but what emerged only in the staging was the impact of Antony's exit. His first offer to go ("Away, my Thetis!" 60) is interrupted by the entrance of the soldier with his six lines that start: "O noble Emperor, do not fight by sea, / Trust not to rotten planks" (61–62). Antony's subsequent exit line is then "Well, well, away" (67).[13] Given the focus on the tug-of-war, what seems to a casual reader a throw-away phrase of little importance became an opportunity for the actor to look at the three Romans stage right at the first "well," then back at Cleopatra on the second, then depart. What turns out to be a disastrous choice could not have been clearer. Generations of readers may have noted the Rome versus Egypt dichotomy in Antony's choices and the play as a whole, but staging the scene in a post-allegorical mode sharpened the focus and gave added weight to the dynamics of this choice.

Arresting the Vice

A second legacy of the late moral drama is linked to ways of structuring the elements and action of a play. Most scholarly formulations draw upon early moral plays such as *The Castle of Perseverance*, *Mankind*, and *Everyman* and focus on the Humanum Genus protagonist and the *psychomachia* tug-of-war for his soul, but to dwell primarily upon this line of descent is to oversimplify the evidence and to ignore the Vice, the predominant figure in English drama in the generation before Marlowe and Kyd. The emergence of the Vice as the central figure in the interludes of the 1560s and 1570s represents a practical theatrical answer to the problem of how to present onstage a critique of what is wrong in society. Playgoers were regularly confronted with a lively, often very funny figure that sets up a special bond with his audience and then acts out with wit, energy, and comic violence the power of some corrupting force (Courage, Covetousness, Haphazardness, Inclination, Ill Report, Infidelity, Iniquity, Newfangledness, Revenge) only to be defeated or transcended in the play's final movement. At some point almost every Vice wields his dagger with comic bravado against foes or allies, but ultimately he is thwarted, in some cases by an opposing figure wielding a sword of Justice. Quite a few plays, then, exhibit a consistent pattern: a jesting Vice, who embodies a force that threatens society as a whole, brandishes his dagger of lath and has his moments of fun and dominance (while one or more victims are led into sin), only to be arrested or eclipsed in a second climactic movement that brings him, his weapon, and what he has come to represent under control. For playwrights like Marlowe and Shakespeare this way of structuring a play narrative would have been as familiar as the Humanum Genus-centered approach or, for today's reader, the pattern of action taken for granted in a cinematic western, a situation comedy, or a detective story.

Of particular interest for later drama is the mechanism by which the Vice is contained or defeated in a play's final movement. Later allusions indicate that the best-known disposition of the Vice was to have him carried off to Hell on the Devil's back, but that choice is found in only one extant moral play, Ulpian Fulwell's *Like Will to Like* (1568): "*He rideth away on the Devil's back*" (1301).[14] In John Pickering's *Horestes* (1567) after a string of successes the last appearance of the Vice Revenge is as a beggar "*with a staff and a bottle or dish and wallet,*" a "sudden mutation" that he attributes to the arrival of Amity who "is unto me Revenge most contrary. / And we twain together, could not abide" (1233, 1254, 1258–59). The figure that had dominated the action is transformed into a beggar, denied his original power, and replaced by allegorical opposites (Truth and Duty) who provide the remedy to his threat. Elsewhere, two Vices are countered by means of fire. At the climax of *King Darius* (1565) with Iniquity outnumbered by the virtues, the stage direction reads: "*Here somebody must cast fire to Iniquity,*" and his exit line is: "Nay, I go to the devil, I fear" (pp. 78–79). In *The Cobbler's Prophecy* (1590) Contempt, albeit not specified as a Vice, clearly embodies "envy and dissension among the several estates and for the resultant turmoil and injustice in the realm."[15] Although this allegorical prime mover is never punished, the curing of the kingdom is effected when the Duke, his daughter, the Priest, and the Scholar repent, pledge reformation (humility for pride, obedience for presumption, love for contempt, and chastity for lust) and then burn the cabin of Contempt: they "*compass the stage, from one part let a smoke arise: at which place they all stay*"; "*They all kneel down*"; "*They all rise and cast incense into the fire,*" at which point they get news of peace and victory (1565–66, 1571, 1589).

In the majority of extant plays, however, the Vice is *arrested* in both senses of the term: "The act of stopping anything in its course; a stop put to anything, stoppage, stay, check" and "The apprehending or restraining of one's person, in order to be forthcoming to answer an alleged or suspected crime" (OED II.5, 8). In *Nice Wanton* (1550), Iniquity (not specifically designated as the Vice) tempts and corrupts two figures, Dalilah and Ismael. In the climactic trial scene, when Iniquity is implicated as Ismael's accomplice, the allegorical figure threatens: "He that layeth hand on me in this place: / Shall have my brawling iron laid on his face" and the stage direction reads: "*They take him in a halter and he fighteth*" (B4r). The same figure that had dominated the two protagonists in the first phase of the action is now literally and figuratively arrested, so that his threats no longer carry any force. Similarly, Inclination in *The Trial of Treasure* (1567) can be bridled early in the play by Just and Sapience, but, confident that his victim, Lust, will release him, the Vice assures us: "though that I be bridled a while, / The colt will at length the courser beguile." At the climax of the play, however, Just leads in a struggling Inclination "*in his bridle shackled*" and even tightens the reins. Although the Vice promises to "rebel, yea, and rebel again," he is led off to prison under control, an exit juxtaposed with the display of the fates of Lust and Treasure (turned to dust and rust) and the awarding of the crown of Felicity to Just (pp. 280, 297, 299). The continuing threat posed by man's "beastly inclination" is both placed in a larger salvific framework and linked to a recurring bridle-snaffle-shackle image that provides a theatrically visible answer to the Vice's energy and threat.

In *Horestes* and also in the better-known *Cambyses* the Vice can be incorporated into a well-known story. In Thomas Garter's *Virtuous and Godly Susanna* (1569) the Vice Ill Report is instrumental in getting the two judges to condemn the heroine; later, after Daniel appears as judge, the Vice helps to lead the two false judges to execution while continuing to serve as chief comedian. But with the appearance of his opposite, True Report, the Vice's wit and comic energy lose their punch. Rather, the formerly successful comic violence and disruption now are brought under control: "*Here they struggle together, the Gaoler casts the Rope about Ill Report's neck*" (1367–68). Instead of going directly to Hell, the Vice is taken off to be hanged, and the Devil enters to forecast Ill Report's fate in Hell. Again, the same figure that had controlled the action (and entertained the playgoers) throughout much of the play is judged, arrested, and taken off for hanging in a final phase characterized by an ideal judge, Daniel, and the Vice's symbolic opposite, True Report.

Similarly, the Vice Haphazard in *Apius and Virginia* (1564) epitomizes not only a weakness to which Apius is susceptible but also an amoral attitude (roughly defined as "take a chance—perhaps you may get what you want") that pervades the world of the play. But after Apius has been condemned by Justice and Reward, the Vice spells out his distinctive rationale one last time in a long speech (1081–1115) in which he decides to ask for his reward, reasoning: "the worst that can hap is but a no" (1106). But the same "haphazard" approach that earlier had seduced Apius now yields the "reward" of a rope, so that although the Vice tries "*to go forth*," he is forced to "stay a while" (1142–43) and eventually is led off by Virginius to be hanged. The final speeches of Fame, Memory, Justice, and Reward then stress how Virginia's death "shall ever reign / Within the mouth and mind of man, from age to age again" (1194–95) as opposed to the short-term power of Haphazard that has been transcended in this final movement of the play.

The presence of both the Vice and various allegorical alternatives in a world also populated by figures like Susanna, Horestes, and Apius may jar the sensibilities of readers today who view such a combination as evidence of the primitive nature of English drama before the triumph of realism. Yet despite their limitations, these renditions of famous stories show how early Elizabethan dramatists were able to use the Vice both as an entertainer *and* as an allegorical index to the central issues of the play. Equally revealing, the final phase of each rendition is clearly linked to the fate of the Vice, so that the diminution or arrest of this formerly dominant figure is brought about by allegorical opposites (True Report in *Susanna*; Amity, Truth, and Duty in *Horestes*; Reward and Justice in *Apius*) who epitomize the new situation at the end in a manner analogous to the climaxes of plays such as *Wealth and Health*, *King Darius*, and *The Trial of Treasure*. The Vice and this two-phased movement were available as a formula that could be adapted to various ends, including the presentation of well-known stories not closely associated with the moral play.

The most revealing example of this formula is to be found in George Wapull's *The Tide Tarrieth No Man*, where Courage the Vice controls the action throughout the first two-thirds of this play in contrast to the plight of "deformed" Christianity. In the final scene, however, the Vice is arrested by Correction in the presence of Authority, a figure who bears "this sword of God's power" (1837). In typical fashion, Courage resists, but here the same dagger that earlier had dominated the action fails to protect its wielder when juxtaposed with the sword of God's authority and the correction that accompanies it. Then, once the Vice has been taken off under arrest, Faithful Few can restore Christianity's sword of Truth and shield of Faith to their pristine state, the culminating action of the play. The formula implicit in other moral plays is here spelled out and fully realized in terms of two sets of weapons, two contrasting powers, and two phases of the action that, taken together, present one moral thesis.[16]

The significance of the Vice's arrest is enhanced by an earlier scene. According to the information presented on the title page, in the middle of this play the actor playing the Vice must exit to reappear moments later as the poor but honest Debtor who refuses to bribe the Sergeant and therefore is led off to prison while wealthy figures like Greediness and No Good Neighborhood bend the law. Despite its obvious point about the corrupt world, this brief scene may seem gratuitous to a modern reader—at least until that reader links it to the final movement when Courage tries to flee from Faithful Few and Authority (who carries a sword and is addressed in judicial terms) only to be grasped by Correction who is told: "thine office do, / Take here this caitiff unto the jail" (1813–14). Clearly, in function (if not in costume as well), Correction is a positive or heavenly version of that corrupt sergeant who led off the impoverished debtor (with the latter role performed by the same actor now portraying the Vice—his only such double in the play). As with the deformed versus restored Christianity, the spectator is offered two stages in a process that structures the entire play—the movement from the domination of the Vice and his worldly interpretation of the proverbial title (*carpe diem*) to the emergence of Faithful Few and Christianity with their heavenly version of the same proverb (see lines 43–49). The importance of the role played here by Authority and Correction, moreover, is reinforced by the account of a lost play, *The Cradle of Security*, which also climaxed with the appearance of two old men, "the one in blue with a Sergeant at Arms, his mace on his shoulder, the other in red with a drawn sword in his hand"—figures identified as "the end of the world, and the last judgment."[17]

Arresting Doll Tearsheet

To turn to the drama of the 1590s and thereafter is to find plentiful examples of arrests and incarcerations without overt allegory, examples not limited to the final sequence of a given play. Such actions can be a source of comedy, as in *The Comedy of Errors* where ten of the fifteen dialogue uses of *arrest* and its variants occur in 4.1 and 4.2. Sometimes a positive, as opposed to a Vice-like, figure is arrested (as with the hapless Debtor in *The Tide Tarrieth*): Duke Humphrey in *2 Henry VI*, 3.1; Antonio in *The Merchant of Venice*, 3.3; Antonio in *Twelfth Night*, 3.4; Posthumus in *Cymbeline*; Hermione in *The Winter's Tale*. Such situations can be complex, as with the arrest of Carlisle in *Richard II* ("of capital treason we arrest you here" 4.1.151) after his prediction of the horrors to come as a result of the deposition (a vision that can be arrested but not forestalled) or with the taking into custody of Celia and Bonario in *Volpone*, an action that epitomizes the vulnerability of Justice in Venice owing to the machinations of Mosca and Volpone. Less common is a figure successfully resisting arrest, as in *2 Henry VI*, where the "good" Duke Humphrey is arrested, then murdered in Act 3, but the plotting duke, Richard of York, refuses to comply with his arrest in Act 5 ("he is arrested, but will not obey" 5.1.136), thereby setting up the first battle of the Wars of the Roses.[18]

Of particular interest are situations in which a figure that epitomizes what is wrong in the world of the play is arrested (again, in both senses of the term) in the final movement: Borachio, Conrade, and Don John; Falstaff and his companions; Angelo and Lucio; Iago and Othello; and Edmund. The adaptation of the moral drama arrest for structural purposes is best seen in *2 Henry IV*. Of the four examples of "arrest" in the dialogue, three are linked to Fang and Snare's failed attempt to arrest Falstaff on behalf of Mistress Quickly (2.1.8, 45, 70–71). The fourth is found after the rebels, believing Prince John's "princely word," have dismissed their soldiers at Gaultree Forest, at which point Westmoreland announces to Hastings: "I do arrest thee, traitor, of high treason" (4.2.66, 107). In the first instance neither the Lord Chief Justice (in both 1.2 and 2.1) nor the would-be arresters can bring Falstaff under control; in the latter instance the rebel leaders *are* arrested but the problems facing the sick king and the sick kingdom are not resolved by this arrest. In contrast, in Act 5, under a new king and a newly empowered Chief Justice, Falstaff and his companions (including perhaps Justice Shallow) *are* arrested and contained (to the displeasure of generations of readers and playgoers). In Part 2 more than in Part 1 Falstaff has been associated with the diseases of the kingdom, so that his arrest, epitomized in the famous (or infamous) rejection speech is linked to the "new" society under Henry V.

The arrest of Falstaff in Part 2 does bear a general debt to the fate of the moral play Vice, but, in terms of Shakespeare's adaptation of the techniques of the previous generation, a more telling example is found in the previous and often neglected scene, the arrest of Doll Tearsheet and Mistress Quickly. To see the connection, an overview of some key motifs is necessary.

Throughout his history plays Shakespeare has often concentrated our attention upon children, heirs, and descent, with Prince Hal and his brothers being but one of many such sets reaching back to the sons of Edward III. Part 2 starts with the reported death of a son, Hotspur, that elicits a reaction from his father that has ominous implications for the future health of the kingdom, followed by the appearance of the son of Richard II's Mowbray, a son who through his presence and pointed comments (see especially 4.1.111–27) recalls the conflicts still simmering from Bolingbroke's past, and by the appearance of a crown prince who waits in the background and discusses his problematic status with Poins in 2.2. Related references recur in the dialogue, whether in the rebels' concern "that our hopes (yet likely of fair birth) / Should be still-born" (1.3.63–64), Mowbray's allusion to the lives that have "miscarried under Bullingbrook" (4.1.127), or the account of fearful omens that include "Unfather'd heirs and loathly births of nature" (4.4.122).

The most revealing passages are linked to the rhetoric of rebellion, especially when the insurgents describe the vulnerability of Henry IV. In one of his major speeches the Archbishop analyzes the awkward dilemma of the king who "hath found to end one doubt by death / Revives two greater in the heirs of life" (4.1.197–98). In this view, each corrective action by Henry IV or his agents instead of providing a solution only adds to the problem (as epitomized by the onstage presence of a second Mowbray). Linking correction, marriage, and children to the more familiar garden imagery, the Archbishop then sums up the dilemma of a king who knows full well he cannot "precisely weed this land." Rather:

> His foes are so enrooted with his friends
> That, plucking to unfix an enemy,
> He doth unfasten so and shake a friend,
> So that this land, like an offensive wife
> That hath enrag'd him on to offer strokes,
> As he is striking, holds his infant up
> And hangs resolv'd correction in the arm
> That was uprear'd to execution. (205–12)

Similarly, just before the rebels accept Prince John's offer, Hastings predicts that if this rebellion fails, others will "second our attempt," and, "if they miscarry, theirs shall second them," so that, in his terms, "success of mischief shall be born / And heir from heir shall hold his quarrel up / Whiles England shall have generation" (4.2.44–49). Although John rejects Hastings's vision of the future ("you are too shallow, Hastings, much too shallow, / To sound the bottom of the after-times" 50–51), the king too is conscious of the problem posed by both current rebels and their heirs in "the after-times." In his final speech to his son he admits that the "soil" attached to his achieving the crown has "daily" led "to quarrel and to bloodshed / Wounding supposed peace," for despite all his efforts to answer the many challenges, he recognizes that "all my reign hath been but as a scene / Acting that argument." But the shrewd Henry IV also recognizes that, since his own death now "Changes the mood," the answer lies in his son: "what in me was purchas'd / Falls upon thee in a more fairer sort; / So thou the garland wear'st successively" (4.5.189–201). The dying king knows that in his own person he can never resolve the continuing problem enunciated by Hastings and the Archbishop. Only a new untainted king, a son who has gained the crown or garland "successively" (rather than "as an honor snatch'd with boist'rous hand" 191), can weed England's garden.

In Act 5 and thereafter Henry V must come to terms with this problem. To show this process in action Shakespeare provides a series of linked moments climaxing in the famous rejection scene. One of these moments, however, has received little or no attention, in these or any other terms. In the brief 5.4, one or more beadles drag onstage Doll Tearsheet and Mistress Quickly, with the accusation against Doll that "There hath been a man or two kill'd about her" and "the man is dead that you and Pistol beat amongst you" (6, 16–17). Meanwhile, the Hostess provides her characteristic comments, including what could be a topic sentence for this final sequence: "O God, that right should thus overcome might!" (24–25). Though Doll rages and the Hostess invokes the name and supposed influence of Falstaff (11), these two figures are arrested, as we are reminded in the next scene just before the rejection when Pistol reveals Doll's fate to Falstaff who promises: "I will deliver her" (5.5.39).

What is particularly striking for the playgoer, moreover, is the stage picture of an apparently pregnant Doll who claims "and the child I now go with do miscarry, thou wert better thou hadst strook thy mother, thou paper-fac'd villain!" (8–10). Given the various rebel allusions to heirs and unborn children, including the Archbishop's image of a wife who holds her infant up to avoid correction, Doll's claim is certainly consistent in metaphoric terms. But in response to this threat of impending miscarriage, the beadle answers: "If it do, you shall have a dozen of cushions again; you have but eleven now" (14–15). The "child," it appears, is only a cushion, another Falstaff-like trick (as with those used against the Lord Chief Justice, Prince Hal, Justice Shallow, or Mistress Quickly) to sidestep authority and the implications of one's actions.

Significantly, in this equivalent to phase two of a moral play the stratagem does not work. In the context established by the rebels' speeches and imagery, not only are Doll and her accomplices arrested in the legal sense (as the rebels were arrested or attached by Westmoreland), but, in addition, their way of life and, even more important, their seeds for the future are also being brought under control. Just as many a Vice or other fallen figure had been arrested by a figure of Correction or Authority (as in *The Tide Tarrieth No Man* and *The Cradle of Security*), so this epitome of the diseases and subterfuges of the world under Henry IV is here being exposed, arrested, and metaphorically denied any progeny. In imagistic terms, an answer under Henry V for the diseases linked to the kingdom under Henry IV (as set forth in Hastings's prophecy that "heir from heir shall hold his quarrel up / Whiles England shall have generation") is being acted out, for, in the Archbishop's terms, "resolved correction" has transcended the threat of the infant hostage or the continuing problem posed by "the heirs of life." Granted, the arrest of the two women is comic, even anarchic, in its language and action, but, especially with the paradigm of the two-phased moral play in mind, there is a logic to both the arrest and the exposure of the false pregnancy that (along with the arrests in the final scene) defines the "new" world under Henry V.

To link a Shakespeare play to a plot or staging convention found in the 1560s and 1570s may not be a startling breakthrough—and I am not advancing the earlier material as a source for the latter. Rather, my goal is to call attention to the common ground beneath the mode of presentation or theatrical vocabulary, a continuity as opposed to a sharp break.[19]

In conclusion, I return to the workshop with psychomachia scenes described earlier and the rationale provided by dramaturge Noam Lior. "These plays, like tracks of music, are composed of multiple layers which present themselves to an audience as a simultaneous experience. Moral allegory, historical reference, psychological realism, and other elements all blend together, in the way that vocals, bass, rhythm, and melody are layered to produce a symphonic experience." The goal of the workshop, he argues, was "not so much try to reconstruct that original melody as to turn up the gain on a single layer—Moral Allegory—to allow it to be heard over and above all the others." In keeping with the arguments and context provided by Brljak and Belsey, my goal has been to tease out more of that residual layer that may have been part of the original playgoing experience. The fundamental question remains: to what extent is a carry-over from the moral-allegorical theatre to the drama of Kyd, Marlowe, and Shakespeare (and thereafter) the norm rather than the exception? Can Every Scholar find Truth in the Kingdom of Theatre History?

Works Cited

R.B. *Apius and Virginia*. Edited by Ronald B. McKerrow. Malone Society. London: Oxford University Press, 1911.

Belsey, Catherine. "Continuity and Change on the English Popular Stage." *Renaissance Drama* 45 (2017): 141–60.

Brljak, Vladimir. "The Age of Allegory." *Studies in Philology* 114 (2017): 697–719.

Dessen, Alan C. *Recovering Shakespeare's Theatrical Vocabulary*. Cambridge: Cambridge University Press, 1995.

Dessen, Alan C. *Shakespeare and the Late Moral Plays*. Lincoln: University of Nebraska Press, 1986.

Fulwell, Ulpian. *Like Will to Like*. In *Two Moral Interludes*. Edited by Peter Happe. Malone Society. London: Oxford University Press, 1991.

Garter, Thomas. *The Most Virtuous and Godly Susanna*. Edited by B. Ifor Evans and W. W. Greg. Malone Society. London: Oxford University Press, 1937.

Harbage, Alfred. *Annals of English Drama, 975–1700*. Revised by. S. Schoenbaum. London: Methuen, 1964.

King Darius. In *Anonymous Plays*. 3rd Series. Edited by John S. Farmer. Early English Drama Society. London, 1906. Reprinted New York: Barnes and Noble, 1966.

Nice Wanton. Edited by John S. Farmer. Tudor Facsimile Texts. Amersham, 1908.

Pickering, John. *Horestes (The Interlude of Vice)*. Edited by Daniel Seltzer. Malone Society. London: Oxford University Press, 1962.

Sanders, Wilbur. *The Dramatist and the Received Idea*. Cambridge: Cambridge University Press, 1968.

Shakespeare, William. *The Riverside Shakespeare*. Edited by G. Blakemore Evans. Revised edition. Boston and New York: Houghton Mifflin, 1997.

Spivack, Bernard. *Shakespeare and the Allegory of Evil*. New York: Columbia University Press, 1958.

Thompson, E.N.S. "The English Moral Plays." *Transactions of the Connecticut Academy of Arts and Sciences* 14 (1910): 291–414.

Thorp, Willard. *The triumph of realism in Elizabethan drama, 1558–1612*. Princeton Studies in English, no. 3. Princeton: Princeton University Press, 1928.

Trial of Treasure. In *A Select Collection of Old English Plays Originally Published by Robert Dodsley in the Year 1744*. Edited by W. Carew Hazlitt. 4th edition. Vol. 3:257–301. London, 1874.

Tuve, Rosemond. *Allegorical Imagery: Some Mediaeval Books and Their Posterity*. Princeton: Princeton University Press, 1966.

Wapull, George. *The Tide Tarrieth No Man*. Edited by Ernst Ruhl. *Shakespeare Jahrbuch* 43 (1907): 1–52.

Williams, Raymond. *Marxism and Literature*. Oxford and New York: Oxford University Press, 1977.

Willis, R. *Mount Tabor*. In *REED: Cumberland, Westmoreland, Gloucestershire*. Edited by Audrey Douglas and Peter Greenfield. Toronto: University of Toronto Press, 1986. 362–64.

Wilson, Robert. *The Cobbler's Prophecy*. Edited by A. C. Wood and W. W. Greg. Malone Society. London: Oxford University Press, 1914.

Notes

1. Tuve, *Allegorical Imagery*, 218.
2. Brljak, "The Age of Allegory," 698, 708, 717, 714.
3. According to Thorp, "Before plays could be written which would show men as they are, writers had to believe that this was a better thing to do than to show them as the church or any other regent of morals thought they should be" so that his goal was to show "the decline of didacticism in theme and plot and the consequent triumph of realism" (vii–ix).
4. Belsey, "Continuity and Change on the English Popular Stage," 146–47, 150, 160.
5. For a full exploration of this term see my *Recovering Shakespeare's Theatrical Vocabulary*.
6. In his *Marxism and Literature* Williams distinguishes among dominant, emergent, and residual elements in a given culture. "The residual," he argues, "has been effectively formed in the past, but it is still active in the cultural process, not only and often not at all as an element of the past, but as an effective element of the present. Thus certain experiences, meanings, and values which cannot be expressed or substantially verified in terms of the dominant culture, are nevertheless lived and practised on the basis of the residue—cultural as well as social—of some previous social and cultural institution or formation," 122.
7. Citations are from the 1997 revised edition of *The Riverside Shakespeare*.
8. E. N. S. Thompson, "The English Moral Plays," 315.
9. A notable exception is *Herman's Head*, a sit-com that ran for three seasons (1991–94) on the Fox Network. The protagonist, Herman Brooks, is a fact-checker at a magazine who faces a wide range of romantic and professional problems. What makes the show distinctive is the visible presence of four figures who in their interactions represent four phases of his personality: Angel (Sensitivity, the Female), Animal (Lust, Hunger), Wimp (Anxiety), and Genius (Intellect). For this item I am indebted to Professor Jody Enders.
10. *The Dramatist and the Received Idea*, 217.
11. Dates attached to plays are for the convenience of the reader and are taken from *Annals of English Drama, 975–1700*. With several of the moral plays I have modernized the old spelling.
12. See the attached photo of "Banishing Despair" with Faithful Few (Laine Zisman Newman), Wastefulness (Paul Babiak), and Despair (Adam Lazarus).
13. The exclamation point after *away* provided by the Riverside editor (not in the Folio) obscures an important option for the actor and has been ignored here.
14. For allusions to this stage business see Dessen, *Shakespeare and the Late Moral Plays*, 20–21.
15. Spivack, *Shakespeare and the Allegory of Evil*, 210.
16. For a fuller account of such two-phased moral plays see chapter 2 of Spivack, *Shakespeare and the Allegory of Evil*.
17. For the full passage see *REED: Cumberland, Westmoreland, Gloucestershire*, 362–64.
18. Other senses of arrest cited in the OED are also found in Shakespeare's plays: "To seize (property) by legal warrant" (III.12) is used in *Merry Wives*, 5.5.115 ("his horses are arrested for it"); and "To take as security" (III.13) is used in *Measure for Measure*, 2.4.133–34 ("let me be bold. / I do arrest your words") and *Love's Labors Lost*, 2.1.159. The arresting of speech is also found in Collatine's lament over the body of Lucrece: "The deep vexation of his inward soul / Hath serv'd a dumb arrest upon his tongue" (*Rape of Lucrece*, 1779–80). The best known metaphoric-allegorical usage occurs in *Hamlet*, 5.2.336-37 ("this fell sergeant, Death, / Is strict in his arrest"), and the same conceit is found in Sonnet 74 which begins: "But be contented when that fell arrest / Without all bail shall carry me away."
19. In terms of continuity, *A Warning for Fair Women* with its pivotal allegorical dumb shows was part of the repertory of Shakespeare's company, the Lord Chamberlain's Men, in the late 1590s.

Tom Tyler and His Wife: Allegory, Satire, Shrews and Sheep

Dana L. Key and Emma Whipday

The late Tudor interlude *Tom Tyler and his Wife* was published in 1661 as the second (and only extant) edition of "Tom Tyler and His Wife, an excellent old play, as it was printed and acted about a hundred years ago."[1] It stages the rebellion of Strife, a shrewish wife, against the authority of her husband Tom Tyler, and his failed attempts to tame her. Strife joins with two other women, gossip Sturdie and the alewife Typple, in convivial misbehaviour—drinking, singing, gossiping, dancing—in what seems to be a positive, if transgressive, model of female community, yet Strife also beats her husband so badly that even her friends disapprove. Her husband Tom Tyler seems to be a victim of his wife's tyrannical household rule, but in attempting to tame his wife, he enlists the violent help of another man, Tom Taylor (referred to hereafter as Taylor). Taylor impersonates Tom Tyler by assuming his coat, and beats Strife until she is near death; when Strife learns of her husband's cowardly trickery, she beats him again. Allegorical figures, Destiny and Patience, have to become involved, and even they can offer no easy answers as to how to solve an unhappy marriage (we will use "she/her" to discuss these figures, as iconographically, they were usually portrayed as female).

This play rehearses common sixteenth-century platitudes about bad marriages, while drawing on a rich vernacular tradition of comic portrayals of violent wives and insufficient husbands, and calling the shrew-taming narrative into question, by complicating our understanding of what is at stake, and who is at fault. The existing criticism on the play is brief, and often only considers it in relation to its more famous shrew siblings—Shakespeare's *The Taming of the Shrew* (as it appears in the Folio), and the anonymous *The Taming of a Shrew* (which may be a source for, or an adaptation or memorial reconstruction of, Shakespeare's play).[2] For example, Janet Clare writes of *Tom Tyler and his Wife*:

Ultimately, husband and wife are made to mend their ways by the intervention of Patience, who tells them she 'cannot abide' domestic disharmony. . . . *A Shrew* and *The Shrew* are far more sophisticated interventions into such proverbial lore.[3]

This article suggests that *Tom Tyler and his Wife* is in fact an equally sophisticated intervention in proverbial lore. It draws on and reimagines older dramatic conventions, featuring allegorical figures and a morality play structure. In situating recognisable village character types alongside the more familiar abstractions of Desire, Destiny and Patience, it embodies a shift from an explicitly religious to a social, secular morality tradition, in its emphasis on the extent to which marital transgressions are embedded in, and abetted or countered by, a wider community of watching neighbours. Furthermore, in staging an attempted, violent taming of an authoritative wife by a brutal neighbour who lacks the marital right to strike her, in disguise as, and commissioned by, her overawed and cowardly husband, *Tom Tyler* forces the audience to confront the extent to which the act of taming implies a husband's failure, and to ask whether legally and religiously condoned marital violence is a form of assault.

In this article, we suggest the significance of this little-studied play to our understanding of the transition between medieval morality play traditions and the emerging social satire characteristic of the early modern genres of domestic comedies, shrew-taming plays, and city comedies. *Tom Tyler* draws upon, and reimagines, a centuries-old tradition of shrewish wives found onstage, on the page, and in visual and material culture; we therefore argue that without a more sustained exploration of the gender politics of this play, our history of staged shrewishness in early modern England is incomplete. We also suggest that such an exploration first requires an understanding of how *Tom Tyler*, as a performance text published about a century after its initial performance context, might function in performance, drawing on our own recent "practice as research" staged reading of the play.

"You shall hear merrie sport": *Tom Tyler* in performance

Evidence supporting the original performance auspices of the play is sketchy. Thomas Colwell entered some "ballettes" of Tom Tyler in the Stationers' Register in April or May of 1563. It is unclear whether this entry may be a reference to the play itself or a ballad contained within the play. Critics over the past century or so have provided little substantive evidence about its original performance history. Fleay stated that the play had been originally acted "either by the Paul's boys or more likely by those of the Chapel." Chambers found Fleay's assertion arbitrary but did not himself offer any firm opinion; he merely restates certain inferences to a boys' company and the Queen from the play's prologue and epilogue and offers the caveat that very many of the interludes and farces in his survey cannot be "absolutely proved to have been given at Court." Martin Wiggins, in his recent compendious catalogue of British drama, also relies upon the prologue to conclude that "the play was written for performance by boys."[4]

There is indeed mention in the prologue that *Tom Tyler* is a "play set out by prettie boyes" and its epilogue contains a prayer for the Queen (presumably Elizabeth) (lines 6; 872–76). However, as Tiffany Stern has demonstrated, prologues and epilogues are not always integral elements of the play itself and were frequently written by another author or appended on a later occasion.[5] While there is no extant evidence to dispute these claims found to date, it must also be noted that there is no evidence to confirm this play was originally performed at Court. Indeed, there are many points to suggest that *Tom Tyler and His Wife* would have been an exceptional play to have been performed at Court around 1561—from the social status of the characters and the contemporary English setting to the small cast size, the lack of elaborate costuming, the simplistic songs, and the use of local idiom and proverbial language—at a time when, the scanty surviving data suggests, many of the plays at court were based on subjects of antiquity.

Without a clear sense of the original performance context, and with an awareness that the play has a flexible dramaturgy without defined settings for scenes, our practice as research staged reading of the play focused upon the performance potential of the text in terms of character and actor-audience relationships, rather than the potential spaces or material conditions of performances. Practice as research provides a corrective to the Shakespearean predominance in the contemporary canon, whereby any Shakespeare play under consideration has been seen in performance in myriad incarnations, on stage and screen, providing a plethora of actor choices, and highlighting the moments where such choices must be made and how the playtext functions in performance: a pertinent example is Katherina's much-discussed submission speech in *The Taming of the Shrew*.[6] In contrast, the majority of non-Shakespearean drama exists only in its textual incarnation, and is therefore at a disadvantage when placed in conversation with Shakespearean works; staging non-Shakespearean drama can highlight dramaturgical features and possible actor choices, while also providing a way of approaching texts that function differently onstage from on the page.[7] Many of the aesthetic qualities that might make some inclined to dismiss or ignore *Tom Tyler*—its plodding rhyming couplets, slapstick violence, use of outmoded allegorical personifications, and delight in proverbial and idiomatic language—can be judged by different standards if it is approached as a performance text.

In our staged reading of *Tom Tyler*, we used selected "original practices" in rehearsal and performance, in order to attempt to replicate key performance conditions from the early modern stage.[8] We borrowed from the "Read Not Dead" staged readings at Shakespeare's Globe, in having actors with scripts in hand, a single group rehearsal, and limited, emblematic props and costumes, focusing on the actor-audience relationship, as enabled by shared or universal lighting; we also included the seven songs required by the playtext—songs which mostly appear, from their use of character names and plot points, to have been written for the play itself, but which probably, as was common, used existing tunes.[9] We encouraged audience members to join in the communal refrains to some of these songs, in keeping with the feast-like or festival atmosphere we aimed to create. Alan J. Fletcher has argued that the "pervasive ale-orientation" of the Tudor comedy *Gammer Gurton's Needle*, first performed at Christ's College Cambridge, requires an appreciation of the beer "toasted onstage in words and action, and doubtless imbibed offstage in reality in the hall":

> [The play] released a social laughter embodied in an organic dramatic enterprise. This project could never expect wholly to survive [publisher] Thomas Colwell's readerly redaction of it a generation later.[10]

The same could be said of *Tom Tyler*: drinking, and singing drinking songs, forms a central plank of the play's plot, and while we performed in a university room rather than in a Tudor hall, we offered audience members refreshments (from wine and mead to pork scratchings, in reference to the "gammon of bacon" that forms an onstage prop), and aimed to promote a social and convivial atmosphere. In so doing, we, like Fletcher, suggest that there is more to *Tom Tyler* than the readerly redaction available in print.

Like the original boy company, we used cross-gender casting; however, our cross-gender casting went in both directions, with the ale-wife, Typple, played by a male actor signalling his gender through emblematic props, such as a scarf over his hair, while Tom Tyler himself was played by a female actor. We hoped that these choices would have an estranging effect, calling into question gender and its implications in a similar way to the original casting, though we were alert to the fact that the resonances of adult actors performing marital strife were very different from those of boy players performing adult relationships.[11] We used cue-scripts, or "actors' parts," with just each actor's own lines and three-word cues, rather than full scripts, building on the research of Tiffany Stern and Simon Palfrey. We wanted to explore how these methods inflected each actor's sense of their own character, the developing character relationships, and our own close readings of the play, in a challenging departure from the Read Not Dead model.[12] In using this rehearsal method, with an onstage bookkeeper, and a very limited rehearsal period, we wanted, as far as possible, to avoid psychological realism, or anachronistic Stanislavskian approaches to character. We were equally keen to avoid realism in the performance of domestic violence, and so we used squeaking plastic truncheons for the beatings, which we hoped similarly estranged the audience from "believing" the violence, in keeping with the play's comic register.

Our practice as research methodology relied on gathering information not just from the rehearsal and performance as experienced by the actors, but also from audience responses gathered through post-performance questionnaires, which asked questions about the relationship between allegorical personifications and human characters in the play; moral messages; audience empathy; and responses to onstage violence. In approaching these responses, we do not attempt to map contemporary audience responses onto an imagined early modern audience—as Sarah Werner puts it, "if it can be difficult to know what today's audiences are doing, it is even harder to ascribe responses to past audiences."[13] Rather, we use contemporary audience responses to explore how the play itself functions in performance, tracing what Andy Kesson calls the "contingent possibilities of a contingently preserved text."[14] Our theatrical close reading of the play, informed by audience responses, will be incorporated into our wider exploration of allegorical characters and gender politics in this significant precursor to Shakespeare's *Shrew* plays.

"I represent the part that men report": Allegorical Personification and Social Satire

Tom Tyler and His Wife borrows certain conventions from late medieval morality drama: firstly, it follows the basic transgression and repentance structure of morality drama and, secondly, it relies on allegorical personifications at a time when playwrights were experimenting with staging more recognizably human characters. Regarding the first point, Lorna Hutson has demonstrated how "Renaissance or post-Reformation theatre has continuities with the sacramental or penitential theatre of the previous century in that it is concerned with the questions of sin, restitution, and forgiveness that were once at the heart of the sacrament of penance."[15] Hutson also argues, however, that post-Reformation humanism prompted a "transformation of penitential culture, as well as of . . . the stagecraft and dramaturgy of penitential theatre" and converted what was a priestly-mediated experience to one more democratic where the ethical judgment rested with the local audience.[16] Indeed, the morality play structure has been adapted by the playwright of *Tom Tyler* in a fresh interpretation that suits his domestic drama: over the course of the play it is reported to the audience how the temptations of Desire led Tom to his unfortunate marriage and his discontent leads him to arrange a ruse whereby Strife is badly beaten in retribution for shrewish ways. Through the intervention of conventional village character types, a gossip and an ale-wife, and the allegorical personification of Patience, the repentance of both husband and wife for their violence is encouraged and the supposed reconciliation of all parties ends the play. The playwright's adaptation of the morality structure, thus, departs completely from religious ideas of sin and instead explores domestic transgression and discord.

This move from the spiritual to the secular *milieu* was increasingly popular among the playwright's contemporaries. Jane Griffiths has argued that:

> The shift from theological to secular concerns might itself be said to mean that the morality's conflicts become less "eternal"; if they are played out in the context of this world rather than the next, they are necessarily finite. Yet more significantly, the drama of this period manifests a striking self-consciousness about the limitations of the mode it deploys.[17]

The second use of convention, the playwright's use of personified allegory, bears witness to how staged allegory was becoming superannuated: the purely allegorical figures, rather than being central characters, have been relegated to the opening and closing scenes of the play. However, mid-century Tudor interludes like *Tom Tyler* often stage characters that occupy a middle ground between the staged personifications of purely abstract qualities (e.g., Lechery or Pride in *The Castle of Perseverance*) whose actions align with the quality signaled by their name, and the more multi-faceted human characters of the late Elizabethan stage, whose interiorities are complex and prompt unanticipated action and plot movement. The playwright of *Tom Tyler* makes use of the older allegorical tradition while self-consciously signalling throughout his awareness of the humor these increasingly outmoded characters can create. Destiny, Desire and Patience all adhere to the older traditions, but Strife, Tom Tyler, Taylor and the gossips Sturdie and Typple anticipate the new type of character that sits between personified allegory and historical person. From Typple, the audience would expect drunken ribaldry and from Sturdie, a contemporary audience might expect a surly demeanor and an intractable nature. Elizabeth Fowler, making an intriguing contribution to the critical lexicon, calls these characters "social persons" by which she means characters who indicate "a paradigmatic representation of personhood that has evolved historically among the institutions of social life."[18] An initial consideration of the playwright's apparent attitude towards the older, conventional figures of personified allegory will help frame an analysis of how he incorporates characters who tend towards more recognizable "social persons" and thus creates moments of vibrant social satire.

Michael Murrin has argued that "Allegory is intimately associated with the society in which the poet writes; it demands human participation and must be explicable in social terms."[19] Therefore, since Destiny, Desire and Patience each personify a purely abstract quality they must behave according to their names, or else their roles lose their allegorical significance for the audience.[20] The playwright betrays his use of allegorical convention when Destiny opens the play with self-descriptive lines reminiscent of pageantry: "I represent the part that men report, / To be a plague to men in many a sort" (1–2). Although Destiny claims she is worthy of neither praise nor dispraise, the dialogue is playfully alluding to convention by stating clearly what her role is in terms of the expectations of an audience well-versed in dramatic allegory. Fulfilling such expectations makes Destiny more plot function than character. The presence of Destiny suggests to the audience that, although the play will provide action and comedy, the conclusion to Tom and Strife's story is self-evident: they cannot escape the marital destiny implied by Strife's name. Indeed, a member of our modern audience found the plot device of the allegorical framework enhanced the delivery of didacticism of the drama: "I really liked the mixing of allegorical and human characters, and thought it was a surprisingly effective way of delivering a moral message."

Desire never directly interacts with the human characters in the play, although Destiny and Patience do. This distance that Desire maintains is itself a departure from the morality format; typically, the figure of temptation would personally goad the protagonist towards bad behavior or an ill-advised liaison. Although we do not see him enacting his role as tempter, the responsibility for the match of Tom Tyler and Strife is claimed in reportage by Desire, who, in a similar manner to Destiny's, boasts about how he played out his role as required by the abstract quality he represents:

> For as for my part, though it long to my Art
> Mens hearts to inflame, their fancies to frame
> When they have obtained, I am not constrained
> To do any more. (54–57)

His part in prompting the plot discharged, Desire quite clearly has no individual agency to exceed the activities circumscribed by his name which is perhaps why the playwright offers no opportunity for his reappearance in the play. However limited in scope in this particular play, Desire as a character reflects the contemporary trend of staging interior qualities of the human mind. Although there was still evidence of the "historical figure" of the devil as the chief Vice figure, for instance, when Satan claims to be the agent for the young man's bad marriage in Thomas Ingeland's *The Disobedient Child* (1560), the agents of temptation in the mid-sixteenth-century interludes are more likely to be abstract personifications of intellectual or emotional states of mind. Similar characters to Desire include Carnal Concupiscence in Lewis Wager's *The Life and Repentance of Mary Magdalene* (*c.* 1560) and Carnal Cogitation in *The Trial of Treasure* (*c.* 1567). Desire, by exiting the play so soon after reporting his success, signals that his quality has been internalized already by the character of Tom Tyler, thereby eliminating the need for Desire to engage in any direct interaction. Conversely, Patience, the incarnation of a morality play character of virtue, makes her appearance towards the end of the play, actively encouraging the warring spouses to internalize her abstract quality and seek to reconcile. Such a peace, however, would require the character of Strife to break free from the allegorical mold of the shrewish wife into which her very name has cast her, drawing attention to the tensions inherent in the shift from the allegorical personification to the more multi-faceted human character capable of such a departure from expectations.

The shrew enjoyed a long tradition in native English drama as the vibrantly embellished account of the Flood in the Chester mystery plays bears witness, to mention just one example. In the Chester play, Noah's truculent wife argues with him and refuses to board his ark, preferring to remain drinking and gossiping with her friends until their sons physically drag her on board, at which point she slaps Noah whilst berating him in a vitriolic verbal attack.[21] Noah's fictional marital woes are prominently depicted elsewhere, such as in stained glass at York Minster as well as Malvern Abbey. Indeed, surviving examples of contemporary iconography attest to the popularity of satirizing the shrew wife character. A number of carved wooden misericords survive from the fourteenth to the sixteenth centuries in cathedrals such as Chester (fig. 1). They often humorously depict shrews beating their men or sometimes a contest between equally violent partners. They can even be found in smaller churches like Stratford-upon-Avon where one misericord depicts marital violence on the left-hand side and one figure being spanked on his bare bottom on the right, reminiscent of Tom Tyler's lament: "For if my wife come, up goeth my bomme" (99) (fig. 2).[22] A late example from Bristol Cathedral (*c.* 1520) depicts a scene whereby a woman attacks a man over a steaming cauldron, pulling at this beard whilst throwing a plate at his head, attesting to the enduring popularity of this type of material satire (fig. 3). Although the violence contained in their carved scenes is strikingly visceral, the great number of examples that are depicted with a touch of humor suggests that late medieval people found amusement in these obstreperous shrews and the opportunities for social satire that they presented.

Figure 1. Chester Cathedral (*c.* 1390). Photo by Dana Key. Used with the kind permission of Chester Cathedral.

Figure 2. Church of the Holy Trinity, Stratford-upon-Avon (*c.* 1466–91). Photo by Dana Key. Used with the kind permission of The Collegiate Church of Holy Trinity with All Saints' Luddington and St Helen's Clifford Chambers.

Figure 3. Bristol Cathedral (*c.* 1520). Photo by Dana Key. Used with the kind permission of Bristol Cathedral.

With such a rich visual and material tradition in mind, it becomes more apparent how the playwright can create a comedy about domestic violence, a concept that sits uncomfortably with our modern sensitivities. True to the form of her iconographic forebears, Strife enters the playing area with gusto:

> I leap and I skip, I carry the whip,
> And I bear the bell; If he please me not well,
> I will take him by the pole, by cocks precious soul
> I will make him to toil, when I laugh and smile. (106–09)

Given the fast-paced action and colorful, colloquial rhythms of the play, it's hardly necessary for the recognizably human characters to announce the relationship of their character to their prominent quality (and name) as Strife does in her opening gambit. However, the playwright perpetuates this convention with each one of the three main characters. The characters of Tom Tyler and Taylor both make reference to the cultural connotations inherent in their names that can be difficult to reconstruct at such a distance, although this article will later explore how long-lasting the popularity of the Tom Tyler character was. In this play, however, he announces himself in a summation of that connotation: "I am a tiler as you see, a simple man of my degree, / . . . I would desire no better life; / Except that God would change my wife" (273; 281–82). Taylor's self-description betrays even more of the playwright's self-conscious recycling of the enduring conventions of popular "social persons," as Fowler has described these figures who personify social relations: "After the old sort, in mirth and jolly sport, / Tayler-like I tell you" (297–98). Without extant evidence to support what personal characteristics were required to be "Tailor-like," perhaps we can infer from his role in the play that Tom Tailors were generally ready for any spirited challenge. Indeed, Tom Tyler and Taylor seem to be doubles of each other, in that they both take up the challenge of shrew-taming, but at the same time are each other's opposite: Tom Tyler is destined to fail and remain browbeaten and Taylor will succeed in taming Strife, if too zealously. Rather than being the personification of a single quality or attribute, Tom Tyler and Taylor, and Strife, satirize commonly found personality types.

When Taylor, accepting Tom Tyler's plea for him to physically chastise Strife into submission, dons Tom Tyler's coat as disguise, the playwright appears to make a subtle jibe at the performance techniques of earlier allegorical drama. It is often noted that one actor could double the roles of Mercy and Tityvillus in *Mankind* (*c.* 1465); David Bevington argues that "Such doubling is striking because it requires the actor to portray his precise opposite . . ."[23] The switch between the portrayal of virtue or vice in these types of doubling scenarios could be effected by a simple two-faced mask or a quick change of coat. The playwright seems to be arguing for the superficiality of such a ruse by asking the audience to believe that Strife would not recognize her own husband by anything other than his coat, thus allowing Tom Taylor to mete out her punishment so successfully. While the changing of one symbolic prop or mask might work for the two-dimensional nature of allegorical personification, the use of such a transparent ruse here, with recognizably human characters, seems to push a touch too hard at the boundaries of the audience's suspension of disbelief.

While Tom Tyler, Taylor and Strife adhere closely to the established conventions for these "social persons," the playwright appears to coax out, and then subvert, any similar expectations the audience would have for the gossip Sturdie and ale-wife Typple. Their early appearances in the play are certainly full of drunken ribaldry and bawdy insinuations in their drinking songs, just as the audience would expect for the fulfilment of their names, but once the audience has gained a comprehensive understanding of Strife's maltreatment of Tom Tyler, the gossips begin to take a different and unorthodox course of action. When, following her beating by Taylor, Strife leaves off contrition and rages with fresh threats of violence, they urge her in sober language to leave off:

> *Strife.* He [Tom Tyler] shall bear me one cuff yet more like a beast.
> *Typple.* Gossip content thee, and strike him no more. (618–19)

This softening of their expected qualities suggests that the playwright departs from a strict adherence to the satire of common village character types and instead encourages deliberation about the ethics of the domestic abuse amongst the members of his audience. By recognizing that Sturdie and Typple are not the extremes of sluttish village debauchery expected of characters akin to John Skelton's Eleanor Rumming and her poetic gossip Alice, the playwright has departed from convention in order to create a situation whereby Strife's actions seem all the worse for her gossips advocating reason.[24]

Indeed, the playwright also creates such dramatic tension by teasing the audience with a potential reversal of the qualities of a shrew through penitential concord. After Strife's vicious beating by Taylor, there is an episode where she seems confused about the retribution, disturbed by the violence inflicted upon her, and quite contrite. It is evident that she simply could not bear the taste of what she had been meting out to her husband. This initial reaction seems closer to how a recognizably human character might react and thus shows the playwright moving towards a type of drama where audience members watch more rounded versions of themselves. While she laments that marrying the weak-willed Tom Tyler might have been her "bane," Tom rightly points out that the catalyst for this whole situation is simply what was required by the cratylic demands of her character: she is Strife and, as he tells her, because of this "the fault was in you" (544; 547).[25] Her contrition doesn't last long; indeed, within thirty lines of dialogue Strife has heard Tom confess his ruse with Taylor and so she resumes her vituperative ranting and threatens Tom with further violent beatings: "Be sure I will pay you, till you do as I would have you / . . . In faith I will plague thee" (591; 597). The moment of potential departure from the shrewish qualities of Strife vanishes in vitriol and the resolution of this tension remains true to her cratylic name: *nomen omen*.[26] Although the attempts at reconciliation explore a greater depth of character whereby Strife could potentially depart from type, the playwright pulls the audience back towards tradition to show how these character types of social satire, while more robust and multi-faceted characters, still share certain cultural and semantic features with personified allegory. By her oath to continue to "plague" Tom Tyler, Strife has internalized Destiny's opening claim "To be a plague to men in many a sort." In so doing, Strife retained her association with the older traditions at a time when playwrights were discovering that the popular figure of the shrew could be better served by creating a human, rather than an allegorical, character.

Jane Griffiths argues that "Many of the [mid-sixteenth-century] plays bear witness to a shift from the assumption that personification allegory is an effective means of 'cloaking' abstract qualities, providing them with a local habitation and a name, to questioning the effectiveness of allegorical representation."[27] Although the appearance of the personified Patience ends the play with another concerted effort towards reconciliation, the original audience were perhaps left wondering whether Strife can be truly rehabilitated and converted into a gentle and loving wife, or whether the cycle will always find her reverting to type as required by her name. Considering the play as a satire of Fowler's so-called "social persons" would suggest the latter, but the playwright nonetheless has experimented throughout with the possibility of permeability in the boundaries delineating the defined qualities and anticipated actions of his character types and started to expose the faultlines that exist in the development of allegorical drama towards social satire. The effect of mingling the two was not lost on our modern audience; one member found that "although the allegorical characters are somewhat flat" they found this was an important plot device in order "to balance out effectively the excessive vitality of the human characters." Although the playwright of *Tom Tyler* still seems ultimately bound by the requirements of older allegorical conventions, these subtle departures that the playwright has made with his "social person" type characters, combined with his self-conscious playfulness with the "old sort" of morality conventions and personifications, strongly suggest an anticipation of the increasing interest in staging the human character, one replete with agency and freedom to develop beyond the strict boundaries delineated by their name. The Katherinas and Marias of the later shrew plays betray through their actions the vibrant traditions of the shrew that helped to inform them, but the drama they inhabit is more complex and the expectations an audience would have for their actions are less transparent because their names allow them the freedom to be more multi-faceted human characters.

The Taming of the Tom, or, Shrews and Sheep

Tom Tyler cast a long shadow. In Fletcher's *Woman's Prize, or The Tamer Tamed* (first performed in *c.* 1611), Maria, newly married to Petruchio, barricades herself within the marital home with some insubordinate women, refusing to allow her husband entry until he agrees to her "conditions" concerning their marriage. The women call down from the "window" on the upper stage to the men gathered below, and "City Wife" boasts of Maria:

> . . . this brave wench, this excellent despiser,
> This bane of dull obedience, shall inherit
> Her liberal will, and march off with conditions
> Noble and worth herself.

Country Wife adds: "She shall, Tom Tylers, / And brave ones, too."[28] The survival of the term Tom Tyler some 50 years after the interlude was first performed suggests the enduring cultural significance of marital dynamics in this little-known play.[29]

Lucy Munro glosses "Tom Tylers" here as "would-be shrew tamers" and discusses the titular Tom's "unsuccessful attempts to subdue" his wife, Strife, while Barry Gaines and Margaret Maurer suggest that "Tom Tyler" became a shorthand for a hen-pecked husband.[30] We suggest a pertinent relationship between these two glosses—Tom Tylers are men who both aim, and fail, to tame their wives, *because* they are, or fear they may become, henpecked husbands. *Tom Tyler* suggests that Tom Tyler is not only a so-called "henpecked" husband—he is also unhappy about it, and his resistance to his subordinate status drives the narrative. When "Country Wife" addresses the onstage male observers as "Tom Tylers, and brave ones, too," she may be referring to the bravery of the Tom Tylers, or to the bravery of Maria's conditions. If the former, she implies the futility of such bravery—their status as would-be shrew-tamers suggests their eventual failure, just as Strife's name, as discussed above, implies her inability to behave as an obedient wife and maintain marital harmony.

In the opening scene, Tom complains of his wife to the audience—she loves:

> To gossip and to swill, when I fare but ill.
> I must work sore, I must get some more,
> I must still send it, and she will spend it . . . (93–95)

In gossiping, drinking, and spending, Strife undoes the prescribed role of an early modern wife.[31] Tom complains, "For if my wife come, up goeth my bomme" (99)—at once a joke on the fact that his wife beats him like a schoolboy (possibly playing on the identity of the actors) and a comment on the fact that the husband who should be at the head of the household hierarchy, is turned upside down by his wife.[32] This is demonstrated by Strife's early declaration to both her gossips and the audience: "Ye should see how I could tame him" (172). Strife does not only refuse to allow her husband's rule, or to expect his anger for her transgressions; she insists on her ability to tame *him*, around fifty years before Fletcher's Maria makes a similar plan—and like Maria, Strife discusses her plans with a community of convivial women, and with the audience.

Strife's taming operates along cross-gendered lines: Tom greets her with a comment on the weather, she accuses him of lying, and when he shares his plan to have a pot of beer and then resume work, she beats him repeatedly for "loitering" when he is paid to work; and threatens to break Tom's head "til the blood go about" if he doesn't "bring her home pence" (194). Strife's violence is prompted by behaviour that would be seen as transgressive if performed by an early modern woman—public speech (she says "yea knave, are you mumbling?") and communal drinking—yet here, it is performed by an early modern man. Strife condemns Tom as if he, and not she, were the errant wife; as Coppélia Kahn puts it, she is "truly a threatening figure because she treat[s] her husband as he normally would have treated her."[33] She at once engages with a fantasy of her husband as stereotypically bad in order to excuse her violence, and treats him, in taming him, as if *he* were a shrewish wife.

After his abashed exit, Strife and her companions celebrate with a song:

> Sturdie:
> Though Tom be stout, and Tom be strong,
> Though Tom be large, and Tom be long,
> *Tom Tiler, Tom Tiler.*
> Tom hath a wife will take no wrong,
> But teach her Tom another song.
> *Tom Tiler, Tom Tiler*
> *More morter for Tom Tiler.* (123–27)

Strife refuses to "take the wrong" that women might expect—that a husband might spend the day's earning on drink[34]—but herself drinks instead, subverting the usual refrain of a drinking song to "teach her Tom another song," calling not for drink, but for "more morter" for Tom, that he might earn the money that she spends in her drinking. These parodic, convivial songs invite the audience to join, perhaps in the refrain, and certainly at laughing at Tom's inability to inhabit the model of the authoritative, pleasure-taking, taming husband, despite his impressive physique—stout, strong, large and long (itself comical when played by a boy actor). His failures as an authoritative husband at once stem from, and make possible, his wife's status as a rebellious shrew.

We can see this failure in Tom's own words. In his opening ballad, he sings:

> I thought when I wed her, she had been a sheep,
> At boord to be friendly, to sleep when I sleep,
> She loves so unkindly, she makes me to weep . . . (68–70)

The image of the ideal wife as a sheep is a significant one. It stems from *Xenophons Treatise of Householde* (1544), Gentian Hervet's translation of Xenophon's *Oeconomicus* from which, as Lorna Hutson observes, the popular "model of husband as hunter-gatherer, and the wife as saver and keeper" is derived.[35] Xenophon's precepts, which became the basis of many Elizabethan conduct manuals, suggest that the education of a wife in household management is the responsibility of her husband:

> A shepe, if it do not well, for the moste part we doo blame the shepherde... And a wyfe like wise, if her housebande teache her well, if she do not followe

> it, she is paraventure to blame. But if he do not teache her, if she be rude, unwomanly, and wytles, is not he to be blamed?[36]

If the wife is not well shepherded, the responsibility lies, at least partially, with her husband. The image is reworked throughout the play—Strife and her gossips sing "Though some be sheep, yet some be shrowes" (667), reminding the audience of their choice to refuse the role of the sheep, and the final, communal song of the play includes the line "To marrie a sheep, to marrie a shrow" (868), offering two contrasting models of wifedom.

The image also occurs in the final lines of the play proper of *The Taming of A Shrew*, printed in quarto in 1592:

> POLIDOR: I say thou art a shrew.
> EMILIA: That's better than a sheep.
> POLIDOR: Well, since 'tis done, let it go. Come, let's in. (xi.166–8)

Emilia corresponds to the "Bianca" character in *The Shrew*; and, like Bianca, she has been discovered to be less obedient than her supposedly curst sister. Here both the accusation (that she is shrewish) and her defence (drawing on the popular proverb "better a shrew than a sheep") are made explicit. As Pamela Allen Brown argues, the existence of this proverb is significant:

> In ballads women use it to criticise wives who let their husbands go whoring; in plays women use it to scoff at the idea of becoming doormats. Outnumbered by misogynist tags geared to men, the proverb offers a tantalising glimpse of an oppositional stance.[37]

In refusing to be cowed by the title of shrew, Emilia does not accept Kate's argument in her submission speech. Furthermore, in using the image of the sheep as a negative one, Emilia refuses to participate in Xenophon's ideal of wives that may be taught like sheep, to represent the good government of their husbands, and calls the shrew-taming the audience have just witnessed into question.

Tom Tyler likewise complicates the conceit of shrew-taming, by presenting the dual culpability of the shrewish wife who refuses to be a sheep, and of the tamed husband who lacks the authority to shepherd his wife. Furthermore, in commissioning his fiery friend Taylor to impersonate him and beat his wife, Tom Tyler undermines his status as pitiful victim, and situates Strife as a potential object of our sympathy. Tyler requests Taylor not only to strike Strife, but to murder her: he wishes to "To live in some blisse, and be rid of my wife" (307).

After Taylor has attacked Strife, Tyler encounters her, with a bandage around her head (505), crying "Alas, alas, I die" (526). This extreme violence was one of the aspects of the play that our audience found most divisive: we aimed to perform the stage violence in a comic register, using squeaking truncheons as props, and yet we could not escape the darker implications of the attack. Strife complains of, and the other characters respond to, the very real effects of the violence on her body: this is no comedy beating, but an attack that means that she cannot rest, she complains that her bones "fall in peeces" (525), and Sturdie and Typple must assist in bandaging her head wound.

Audience comments on the violence ranged from "comical" to "frightening," "acceptable" to "wince" or even "I cried at first"; and many commented that it was "both funny and uncomfortable." One noted that it "started as comedy & quickly became uncomfortable and quite stark domestic abuse—particularly when contrasted with comedy prop of squeaking club"; another that "the Punch and Judy approach was appropriate but didn't trivialise the reality—or our imagination of it"; and another that "the relationship between the story/characters and actors/performance was both playful and disturbing." Those who found it comical or uncomfortable often commented on the (for them imagined) bodies of the boy actors, or on the distance between the onstage action and the language of the playtext; one commented that "the body language was quite metaphorical so it was not problematic." Yet others suggested that their laughter at the comic performance of onstage violence only reinforced their sense of the disturbing and upsetting nature of the violence as described. We suggest that the play sets up a complex dialectic between the comic marital strife performed by boy actors, and the near-fatal violence acted on Strife's body by Taylor; a dialectic that has the potential to prompt a wide range of audience responses, fragmenting an audience rather than uniting them in their engagement with the onstage violence. Indeed, examining the cue-scripts, or "parts," of Taylor and Strife helps to demonstrate the extent to which the onstage, playful bodies of the actors exist in relation to, or in tension with, the violence experienced by the characters in a way that invites diverse responses rather than communal resolution.

Early in the interlude, Strife sets up a power-play based on completing Tom Tyler's rhyming couplets to undermine him: when Tom asks Strife "are you tumbling?" Strife replies "yea knave, leave your mumbling," refusing to allow Tom to inhabit the role of the outraged husband, but rather, inhabiting it herself in chiding him for his speech. Taylor appropriates this tactic in his violence against Strife: when she, believing Taylor to be her husband, asks him if he is "striking," he replies "Yea, whore, are you gleeking," or jibing. He then counters her threats with threats of still worse violence ("I will plague your flesh"), convincing her that he is the stronger ("How like you your match?") in order to force her to inhabit the subject position she has been rejecting—that of the subordinate wife. He succeeds in this when Strife asks him "ah knave, wilt thou strike thy wife," and then reinforces her role with a physical manifestation of it, commanding her to kneel, and ends on a final, grotesquely violent threat: "trouble me never. . . . I will brain thee then." He has succeeded in gaining a position of authority over her in the persona of her husband, a position rooted in his physical strength.

Throughout the scene, the audience must engage in the imaginative work of accepting that Strife is convinced that it is her husband that is beating her, despite the fact that Taylor has done no more than wear her husband's coat. This is a common theatrical convention that nonetheless draws our attention to the seeming interchangability of these two Toms, which reflects the two models of manhood and husbanding they offer: contrasting examples of insufficient and excessive masculinity. As the actor playing Taylor (Oskar Cox Jensen) commented in rehearsal, he offers a character study of what we might now term "toxic masculinity." When his violence escalates Strife asks him to stop, "if thou be a man." The cue-script used by the actor playing Taylor contains only the three cue words—"be a man"—to prompt his response, "Kneel down and ask to be forgiven." The actor playing Taylor would therefore have prepared his line, which asserts his physical dominance, with the cue "be a man" in mind, linking masculinity to the physical dominance he performs:

> ______________________________ be a man
> Kneel down and ask to be forgiven
> ______________________________ bones is sore.
> Ah unhappie whore; do so then no more. (383–86)

In the aftermath of her beating, Strife tries to convince Tom Tyler that his responsibilities as a husband involve the very shepherding that she rejected in refusing the label of "sheep":

> Alas what than, you being a man,
> Should beare with my folly, and you being holly [holy]
> Might councel me, tho not beating me so. (538–40)

Strife's advice suggests that neither Tyler's submission nor Taylor's violence fulfil the ideal of the shepherding husband. But Tom Tyler has chosen an alternative model of masculinity, as offered by Taylor: a model that is dangerously violent and aggressively sexual.

Strife uses the term "knave" to address the man she believes to be her husband, an insult rooted in class distinctions and, potentially, youth. In contrast, as in the example above, Taylor refers to her repeatedly as a whore, suggesting, like so many texts in the period, that Strife's female misbehaviour—drinking, conviviality, insubordination—is linked to sexual transgression. Yet there is no suggestion that Strife commits sexual transgressions; as in Petruchio's taming of Kate, sexualised language here seems to be an element of Taylor's violent taming.

Indeed, like the courtship scene in *The Taming of the Shrew*, Strife's taming by Taylor could be read in terms of mutual attraction: as the actor playing Tom Tyler, Freyja Cox Jensen, commented, the "matching" of Taylor and Strife, as equals, in their verbal sparring, created a sense of pace, compatibility, and sexual tension which was missing from comparable exchanges between Strife and Tyler, suggesting (disconcertingly) that Strife may be attracted to the man who can "master" her, even as this mastery manifests itself in violence. One audience member commented on the "overt connections between violence and erotic excitement. It is very explicit about the way in which brutality is charged by desire, and how there is erotic potential in violence." In the final scene, Patience commands Taylor and Strife to kiss, and Strife comments "I would he had kissed both the ends"—which is perhaps comparable to the moment in Chaucer's *The Miller's Tale* where a kiss of the wrong "end" in the dark is used as a punishment, but which also hints at the possibility of Strife's sexual desire for the neighbour who can "tame" her. This threatened retaliation seems to stem from Taylor's sexualised words and blows; Strife offers an unrepentant, carnivalesque response.

Joy Wiltenburg argues of English broadside ballads that the "violence of English domestic quarrels, especially that exercised by women, is a comic formula out of touch with the possible effects of violence on flesh and bone."[38] Yet such quarrels also present spousal murder as a possible eventuality.[39] Even Shakespeare's *The Taming of the Shrew*, which offers a comparatively non-violent shrew-taming, can be read as suggesting the possibility of eventual domestic murder[40]; Fletcher's *Tamer Tamed* assumes that Petruchio's first marriage to Katherina has ended with her death—and the implication is that he brought about her death himself:

> MARIA: What though his other wife,
> Out of her most abundant stubbornness,
> Out of her daily hue and cries upon him—
> For sure she was a rebel—turned his temper
> And forced him blow as high as she?

Like Fletcher's response to Shakespeare's vision of shrew-taming, or the ballads and plays that stage shrewishness as a precursor to spousal murder, *Tom Tyler* suggests that early modern audiences could well imagine the effects of marital violence upon flesh and bone. Yet *Tom Tyler* incorporates this suggestion within the displacements of a convivial comic framework; displacements that were further reinforced by the "Sly" frame narratives of *A Shrew* and *The Shrew*.

When Strife learns of Taylor's trick, she resumes her beating of her husband, which prompts Patience's entry. Patience apportions blame equally, warning the characters:

> And I would have Tom Tayler to be no rayler,
> Nor Tom Tyler to chide, which I cannot abide.
> Nor his wife for to shew, any prankes of a shrew. (806–08)

Patience's message is one of failure: none of the models of taming the play offers, from Strife's projection of stereotypical husbandly failures onto Tom Tyler, to Tyler's attempt to use trickery to replace his unauthoritative rule with Taylor's aggressive masculinity, results in marital harmony. The failure of this message is a requirement of the allegory; the circular nature of morality play plotting, in which a definite ending can only be reached in the afterlife, requires allegorical characters to continue to perform their earthly natures—whether marital Strife or convivial Typple-ing. Yet in ending with this necessary failure, *Tom Tyler and his Wife* calls into question the very structures of divinely (and socially) ordained domestic authority that those in the play are unable to maintain—albeit within a festival framework of convivial enjoyment of transgressive behavior.

One audience member commented: "At first I thought the whole thing was an intelligent (lovely?) gender inversion until I realized it was just good old-fashioned misogyny with a twist." The playful gender inversion offered by the play is certainly undercut when societal norms are violently reinstated, but we suggest that in its circular structure and its equivocal deus ex machina ending, *Tom Tyler and his Wife* at once reveals its debt to, and subverts, the form of late medieval morality plays, in order to interrogate the misogynistic structures it portrays. In staging this interlude, we were able to explore what, as Alan Fletcher suggests, the "readerly redaction" published in 1661 may miss—how it explores the faultlines of marital hierarchies through playful violence, insufficient stereotypes, and communal song. Fletcher's casual, cutting reference to "Tom Tylers, and brave ones, too," suggests the extent to which this comic vision of shrew-taming, convivial rejections of sheep-like femininity, and violently anxious masculinity, continued (and may continue) to resonate.

Notes

1. Anon., *Tom Tyler and his Wife* (1661) edited by Felix E. Schelling, PMLA 15.3 (1900): 253–89. All further references are to this edition and will be incorporated into the text.
2. See John Jowett, *Shakespeare and Text* (Oxford: Oxford UP, 2007) 75; Barbara Hodgdon, ed., *The Taming of the Shrew* (London: Arden Shakespeare, 2010),

Introduction, 37; and Laurie Maguire, *Shakespearean Suspect Texts: the Bad Quartos and their Contexts* (Cambridge: Cambridge UP, 1996), esp. 308–10.

3. Janet Clare, *Shakespeare's Stage Traffic: Imitation, Borrowing and Competition in Renaissance Theatre* (Cambridge: Cambridge UP, 2014) 97.
4. Martin Wiggins, *British Drama 1533-1642: A Catalogue*, Vol. I (Oxford: OP, 2012) 360–1 (number 340).
5. Tiffany Stern, *Documents of Performance in Early Modern England* (Cambridge: Cambridge UP, 2009) 109-18. For another case study of contested authorship of a court epilogue, see Helen Hackett, "'As the Diall Hand Tells Ore': The Case for Dekker, Not Shakespeare, As Author," *The Review of English Studies* 63:258 (2011): 34–57.
6. See, for example, Barbara Hodgdon, "Katherina Bound; or, Play(K)ating the Strictures of Everyday Life," *PMLA* 107.3 (May, 1992): 538-53.
7. On practice as research as a methodology, see for example Stephen Purcell, "Practice-as-Research and Original Practices," *Shakespeare Bulletin* 35.3 (Fall 2017): 425–43; Dustagheer, Sarah Oliver Jones, and Eleanor Rycroft, eds., "(Re)constructed Spaces for Early Modern Drama: Research in Practice," *Shakespeare Bulletin* 35.2 (Summer 2017): 173–86; Emma Whipday and Freyja Cox Jensen, "'Original Practices and Historical Imagination': Staging A Tragedie Called Merrie," *Shakespeare Bulletin* 35.2 (Summer 2017): 289–307; and Richard Allen Cave, "The Value of Practical Work and of Theatregoing in the Study of Seventeenth-Century Drama (1600–1640)," *Literature Compass* 1 (2003): 1–12.
8. See Callan Davies, *Early Modern Women* 12.2 (Spring 2018), Performance Review: "*Tom Tyler and his Wife*, dir. Emma Whipday, UCL,", 212–18 for production information, including full details of the cast. You can view an archival recording of our staged reading here: www.youtube.com/watch?v=HN5n-BEB6R4&t=601s&frags=pl%2Cwn. We are grateful to the UCL Centre for Early Modern Exchanges and the Leverhulme Trust for their support.
9. These were sourced for our performance by our musical adviser, Oskar Cox Jensen, from William Chappell, *Old English Popular Music* (London, 1838–40).
10. Alan J. Fletcher, "Gammer Gurton's Needle," *The Oxford Handbook of Tudor Drama* edited by Thomas Betteridge and Greg Walker (Oxford: Oxford UP, 2012) 276–92 (289).
11. On the potentially estranging effect of cross-gender casting, see Elizabeth Klett, *Cross-Gender Shakespeare and English National Identity: Wearing the Codpiece* (Basingstoke: Palgrave Macmillan, 2009).
12. Simon Palfrey and Tiffany Stern, *Shakespeare in Parts* (Oxford: Oxford UP, 2007).
13. Sarah Werner, "'Audiences" in *Shakespeare and the Making of Theatre*, edited by Stuart Hampton-Reeves and Bridget Escolme (Basingstoke: Palgrave Macmillan, 2012) 165–89 (p.166). See also Stephen Purcell, *Shakespeare and Audience in Practice* (Basingstoke: Palgrave Macmillan, 2013), esp. 17.
14. Andy Kesson, "Acting out of Character: A Performance-as-Research Approach to The Three Ladies of London," in *Performance as Research in Early English Theatre Studies: The Three Ladies of London in Context* (Hamilton: McMaster University, 2015), threeladiesoflondon.mcmaster.ca/par/AndyKesson.htm.

15. Lorna Hutson, "Theatre" in *Cultural Reformations: Medieval and Renaissance in Literary History*, edited by James Simpson and Brian Cummings (Oxford: Oxford UP, 2010) 227.
16. On neighbourhood self-policing, see, for example Susan Dwyer Amussen, *An Ordered Society: Gender and Class in Early Modern England* (New York: Columbia UP, 1988) 96; Lena Cowen Orlin, *Locating Privacy in Tudor London* (Oxford: Oxford UP, 2007) 10; and Bernard Capp, *When Gossips Meet: Women, Family and Neighbourhood in Early Modern England* (Oxford: Oxford UP, 2003), esp. chaps. 5 and 6.
17. Jane Griffiths, "Counterfet Countenaunce: (Mis)representation and the Challenge to Allegory in Sixteenth-Century Morality Plays," *The Yearbook of English Studies* 38.1/2, Tudor Literature (2008) 17–33.
18. See Elizabeth Fowler, *Literary Character: The Human Figure in Early English Writing* (Ithaca: Cornell UP, 2003) 2. See also Bernard Spivack, *Shakespeare and the Allegory of Evil*, 62–63.
19. Michael Murrin, *The Veil of Allegory: Some Notes Towards a Theory of Allegorical Rhetoric in the English Renaissance* (Chicago: U of Chicago P 1969) 74.
20. See the first chapter in Angus Fletcher, *Allegory: The Theory of a Symbolic Mode* (Princeton: Princeton UP, 2012) 25–69.
21. Surviving evidence shows that the Chester plays were performed from at least 1422, if not earlier, and survived as a Corpus Christi tradition until 1568, overlapping with the estimated date of *Tom Tyler and His Wife*. The plays were copied in manuscript form into the early seventeenth century. See *The Chester Mystery Cycle*, edited by R. M. Lumiansky and David Mills, Vol. I. EETS SS 3 (London: Oxford UP, 1974) ix–xl.
22. See Christina Grössinger, *The World Upside-Down: English Misericords* (London: Harvey Miller, 1976).
23. Bevington, *From Mankind to Marlowe*, 87.
24. See "The Tunnyng of Elynour Rummyng," in *The Complete English Poems of John Skelton* edited by John Scattergood (Liverpool: Liverpool UP, 2015).
25. See Anne Barton, *The Names of Comedy* (Oxford: Clarendon Press, 1990), 7–10.
26. Ibid., 57. Barton discusses these moments of tension in other contemporary plays, particularly William Wager's The Longer *Thou Livest the More Fool Thou Art*. There is an episode in the play where the protagonist, Moros, promises to study diligently and pursue the path of virtue. Moros is condemned to remain a fool, however, by what Barton argues is Wager's adherence to convention and 'the cratylism inherent in morality drama as a form [remaining] still too powerful to be overturned'. This can also be seen in the fleeting repentance of Worldly Man in Wager's *Enough is as Good as a Feast*.
27. Griffiths 19.
28. John Fletcher, *The Tamer Tamed*, edited by Lucy Munro (London: Methuen Drama, 2010), II.v.93–96.
29. This popularity would carry on further still: Thomas Heywood also made reference to the ballad and to "Tom Tiler" as a figure of social satire two of his plays, *The Fair Maid of the West, Part 1* (1631) and *A Woman Killed With Kindness* (1641).

30. Munro, ed., *The Tamer Tamed*, 77; Barry Gaines and Margaret Maurer, eds., *The Tamer Tamed in Three Shrew Plays* ed. (Indianapolis, Indiana: Hackett, 2010) 180.
31. See, for example, similar complaints in Joseph Swetnam, *The Arraignement of Lewd, Idle, Froward and Unconstant Woman* (London, 1615), esp. 1.
32. See Xenophon, *Xenophon's Treatise of the Householde*, translated by Geraint Hervet (London: 1544), and "An Homily of the State of Holy Matrimony," in *Certain Sermons or Homilies Appointed to Be Read in Churches, The Second Book of Homilies* (London, 1571).
33. Coppélia Kahn, *Man's Estate: Masculine Identity in Shakespeare* (Berkeley: U of California P, 1981) 105.
34. See, for example, Martin Parker's broadside ballad *The Married-Womans Case* (London, n.d.), Pepys 1.410–411.
35. Lorna Hutson, *The Usurer's Daughter: Male Friendship and Fictions of Women in Sixteenth-Century England* (London: Routledge, 1994), 21.
36. Xenophon, *Xenophon's Treatise of the Householde*, translated by Geraint Hervet (London: 1544), B2v.
37. Allen Brown 2.
38. Joy Wiltenburg, *Disorderly Women and Female Power in the Street Literature of Early Modern England and Germany* (Charlottesville: UP of Virginia, 1992) 139.
39. See Joannes Bramis, *Here Begynneth a Merry Jeste of a Shrewde and Curste Wyfe* (London, 1580), in which the protagonist beats his horse to death, then threatens the same to his wife.
40. See Whipday, *Shakespeare's Domestic Tragedies: Violence in the Early Modern Home* (Cambridge: Cambridge UP, 2019), ch.1.

Amplificatio in Performance: The Digby *Conversion of St. Paul* on Stage

Ann Hubert

In April 2015, I directed an all-student performance of the Digby *Conversion of St. Paul* at the University of Illinois at Urbana–Champaign.[1] Directing the play provided new insight for me as to how *St. Paul* works as didactic literature. As its name suggests, the *Conversion of St. Paul* explores the religious transformation of its titular character from Jewish Saul to Christian Paul through staging three scenes from the *Acts of the Apostles*. While I knew that Saul started as a proud, powerful man and ended as a humble preacher, staging the play made me realize that Saul is the pivot point through which the play broadcasts and magnifies themes of pride and humility by modeling other characters' behavior on a pre- or post-conversion Saul. This discovery of *amplificatio*, or amplification, certainly clarifies the play's structure; it also heightens the play's intersections with late-medieval sermon practice by revealing an additional way in which the playwright appropriates the arts of preaching.[2] In this article, I will examine how *amplificatio* offers a new rhetorical lens through which to understand the play's thematic and didactic engagement with pride and humility.

Amplificatio refers to a variety of techniques that orators in Antiquity and preachers in the medieval period used to embellish speeches and sermons with important details.[3] In the *Institutio Oratoria*, Quintilian explains that "[*a*]*mplificatio* is a graded enhancement of the basic given facts by artistic means...[and] is served by *res* and *verba*,"[4] where the *res* is "the intellectual topic under treatment" and the *verba* "the linguistic means of expression."[5] He goes on to identify "four main kinds of Amplification, based on Increment, Comparison, Inference, and Accumulation."[6] Quintilian also connects *amplificatio* to *pathos*, stating that the goal of *amplificatio* is to elicit an emotional response from the audience:

> Meanwhile, I content myself with observing that the aim of appeals to the emotions is not only to display the bitter and melancholy nature of troubles that indeed are so, but also to make experiences which are commonly thought tolerable seem grievous: for instance, when we say that there is more injury done by an insult than by a blow, or that disgrace is a heavier penalty than death. The power of eloquence in fact lies not only in driving the judge to the conclusion towards which he will be led by the nature of the facts, but either in arousing emotion which is not there or in making an existing emotion more intense.[7]

Amplification's ultimate purpose, then, is to manipulate an audience's emotions: it both "[makes] the tolerable seem grievous" and "[arouses] emotion which is not there or...[makes] an existing emotion more intense." As I will demonstrate, the *St. Paul* playwright deploys *amplificatio*'s various techniques throughout the play in the careful construction of Saul's ability to stir emotionally not only other characters to the vice of pride but also audience members to the virtue of humility. Presenting Saul's vice and virtue as two sides of the same issue employs what Cicero in the *De Oratore* calls one of *amplificatio*'s commonplaces: "And then there are [other commonplaces of amplification] consisting of double-edged discussions, which offer the possibility of copiously arguing both sides of a general issue."[8] In the *Forma Praedicandi*, Robert of Basevorn identifies this practice as the first method of amplification whereby the definition of a noun is established: "When, however, something is defined or described, the preacher can conveniently make transference to the opposite, because the definition is valid for defining the other."[9] The playwright's portrayal of Saul as pivot point for pride and humility is actually a rhetorical exposition of the connection that this vice and its antidote share, and *amplificatio* is the method through which the playwright transforms Saul into the rhetorical tool announcing pride and humility's correlation. At the start of the play, Saul's visual and verbal claims to power enable characters like the servant, stable groom, and soldiers to imitate and amplify his vice of pride. Conversely, after Saul's conversion, his visual and verbal markers communicate his humility, and his amplification of this virtue through his sermon enables the play's didactic message to reach the audience. Saul as rhetorical tool of amplification ultimately demonstrates that he has learned from his own mistake of pride, a mistake that he acknowledges and rectifies in his sermon, making *amplificatio* a rhetorical technique validating the conversion Saul undergoes.

Part I: Saul's Pride

After Poeta's brief introduction, the *Conversion of St. Paul* immediately establishes Saul's pride through the visual and verbal markers of his power, markers that represent the *res* and *verba* inherent to *amplificatio*. Saul appears to the audience, informing it that he is the "most dowtyd man…lyuyng vpon the ground / Goodly besene wyth many a ryche garlement" (14–15) and peerless: "My pere on lyue I trow ys nott found! / Thorow þe world, from þe oryent to þe occydent, / My fame ys best knowyn vnder þe firmament!" (16–18).[10] The playwright carefully illustrates Saul's power by moving back and forth between a series of superlatives: Saul is the most feared man, the best dressed man, and the man whose reputation is most expansive in the world. The playwright establishes the topic of Saul's power (the *res*) and immediately expands upon it through Saul's verbal bombast and the costumes/props that reinforce his bombast (the *verba*). Each of Saul's verbal claims and physical attributes therefore builds off of the previous one, continuously raising the pervasiveness of his power through Comparison, one technique of *amplificatio*.[11] This technique continues when Saul encounters Caiaphas and Anna; for the abstract "in suernes" (30) and "proteccyon" (42) he seeks to persecute Christians materialize into concrete letters of authority that Anna places in his hands: "And by thes letturs …/ We gyf yow full power so to doo. / Spare not hardly for frend nor foo!" (50, 53–54). The *verba* (the words and props) and the *res* (the topic of Saul's power) again complement each other, reinforcing and elevating Saul's might during his interactions with the high priests. The culmination of the playwright's interweaving of the *res* and the *verba* arrives in the "[f]ull goodly besene" (128) horse on which Saul hastily leaves Jerusalem:

> Here ys a palfray,
> Ther can no man a better bestryde!
> He wyll conducte owur lorde and gyde
> Thorow the world; he ys sure and abyll
> To bere a gentyllman, he [ys] esy and prophetabyll. (122–26)

As well dressed as Saul is, Saul's horse also replicates his rider's worldly reputation, neatly showing how the horse's *res* and *verba* interact as Saul's did to reinforce its status as the best and most powerful. A visual marker of the pinnacle of Saul's power, the horse also visibly marks Saul's sin of pride, of his unchecked ability to act according to his own desire.[12]

Amplificatio establishes Saul's power through the precise crescendo it builds, and the playwright immediately interrogates how this crescendo operates by interpreting it in two different sets of dialogue, first between the servant and stable groom and second between the two soldiers. The interaction between Saul's servant and the stable groom reconfigures Saul's power by locating one aspect of Saul's pride—his impatience to leave and persecute—in his servant and the other aspect—his self-assertion to power—in the stable groom.

At this point in the play, then, the consequence of Saul's pride begins to reveal itself, giving rise to two independent assertions of pride in the wake of one. The interaction begins with Saul's servant becoming increasingly short-tempered at the stable groom's failure to recognize him quickly:

SERUUS: How, hosteler, how! A peck of otys and a botell of haye!
Com of apase, or I wyll to another inne!
What, hosteler, why commyst not thy way?
Hye þe faster! I beshrew þi skynne!

[*The stable groom appears.*]

STABULARIUS: I am non hosteler nor non hostelers kynne,
But a jentylmanys seruuant, I! Þou dost know
Such crabyysh wordys do aske a blow! (85–91)

The servant's imitation of Saul's haste to leave results in a more aggressive and insidious expression of power, as the servant finds himself cursing the man who is supposed to help him prepare for Saul's journey (Saul had no such threatening interactions with the high priests). The imitation of Saul's pride therefore leads to its intensification, an intensification that also extends to the stable groom, who now takes insult at the servant's classification of him as a "hosteler" (89). The stable groom instead asserts that he is, more respectably, "a jentylmanys seruuant" (90), a statement that is of course ridiculous given that he is wearing a well-worn garmet which is likely in tatters and, even if it were not, is not made of materials—"sylk and chamlett" (107)—that would keep him warm:

STABULARIUS: Forsoth, and a hood I vse for to were,
Full well yt ys lynyd wyth sylk and chamlett;
Yt kepyth me fro the cold, þat þe wynd doth me not dere,
Nowther frost nor snow þat I therby do sett.

SERUUS: Yes, yt ys a dobyll hood, and þat a fett!
He was a good man þat made yt, I warant yow—
He was nother horse ne mare nor yet yokyd sow! (106–19)

It is obvious that the stable groom asserts a social status that he does not actually possess,[13] but what is important about his assertion is its failure rhetorically: the stable groom's costume and verbal claims (his *verba*) do not convincingly align with the topic (the *res*) of being a gentleman's servant. What the stable groom's and servant's dialogue replays, then, is the anxiety of recognition latent in Saul's earlier interaction with the high priests: just as Saul was uncertain about whether Caiaphas and Anna would recognize his self-aggrandizement and validate his mission to persecute Christians, so too is the stable groom in this scene eager to have his social standing and purpose recognized and reinforced.[14] Indeed, after approving Saul's plan, the high priests each reaffirm Saul's *verba*, Caiaphas recalling the letters, the props representing Saul's power—"he thus aluay takyth in hande, /...hys power to gouerne thus all thys lande" (145–46)—and Anna recalling the fame, the verbal bombast signaling Saul's power: "Ther ys non such lyuyng vpon þe grownde, / That may be lyke to hym, nor be hys pere, / Be est nor west, ferre nor nere!" (152–54). Saul's servant's unwillingness to do the same for the stable groom reveals that Saul's initial expression of power lies not only in his own ability to amplify it but also in his ability to persuade other characters to amplify it, the latter of which links the playwright's use of *amplificatio* to its chief goal, stirring an audience's emotions. The stable groom is nowhere near as skilled as Saul is as a rhetorician, and in his failure to convince Saul's servant of his social standing, the stable groom shows his inability to use *amplificatio*'s technique of Comparison successfully. The crucial link between *amplificatio* and *pathos* therefore is not forged, causing the servant to continually mock the stable groom rather than be persuaded by him.[15] Where Saul succeeds in using *amplificatio*, the stable groom fails; where Caiaphas and Anna affirm Saul, Saul's servant tears the stable groom down. These interactions highlight how precarious the power won through *amplificatio* can be, a reality that Saul himself will come to grapple with later in the play when God blinds and lames him.

The second reconfiguration of Saul's power and pride occurs between the first and second soldiers. With a handful of exceptions where only the first soldier speaks (120–21, 127–33, 395–97), the first and second soldiers always speak in sequence and they always speak about the same subject matter. Reinforcing each other's ideas through analogous language—a technique of *amplificatio* called Accumulation[16]—the first and second soldiers escalate the expressions of power and pride that Saul introduces into the play. Just as Saul is ready to serve the high priests, so too are the soldiers ready to serve Saul, and their arrogance completely overtakes them as they verbally spar over who takes orders best and who will kill the most rebels, or Christians:

PRIMUS MILES: Vnto your commaundment I am obeysaunce.
I wyll not gaynsay nor make delacyon,
But wyth good mynd and harty plesaunce
I shall yow succede, and make perambulacyon
Thorowoute Damaske wyth all delectacyon.

And all thoo rebell and make resystens,
For to oppres I wyll do my delygens.

SECONDUS MILES: And in me shalbe no neglygens,
But to thys precept myself I shall applye:
To do your behest wyth all conuenyens,
Wythwt eny frowardnes or eny obstynacy—
Non shall appere in me—but, verely,
Wyth all my mynd, I yow insure,
To resyst tho rebellys I wyll do my cure! (64–71)

As with the stable groom and Saul's servant, the soldiers' competitiveness highlights how expressions of pride and power work off of, reinforce, and magnify each other, the playwright now portraying four characters who actively succumb to sin as a result of Saul's rhetoric. These reconfigurations, achieved through Comparison and Accumulation on a word-to-word and sentence-to-sentence level, also work more broadly on a thematic level: as Robert of Basevorn explains, "[w]hen we wish to amplify by means of interpretation, we must consider the different interpretations."[17] In *St. Paul*, each of these four characters are different interpretations of Saul's power and pride, and so *amplificatio* enables the playwright to present four sub-interpretations of pride running rampant in the world. Staging the play's opening sequence therefore revealed how amplification magnifies Saul's pride and clarified the effect of his power: the significance of Saul's power resides not only in his self-assertions to grandeur, as one may expect, but also, and more importantly, in the assertions that this power enables every other character in this sequence to make. However, *amplificatio*'s manifestation of different interpretations does not end in sin or in the first station; rather, its manifestation turns in the play's second and third stations to explore the interpretation of power and pride through humility.

Part II: Saul's Humility

As soon as Saul's power and pride reach their height in his presentation a-horseback en route to Damascus, God easily causes Saul to fall from his horse,[18] a fall that forces Saul to experience fear for the first time: "O Lord, I am aferd, I trymble for fere!" (188). Now both blind and lame, Saul must realize his agency differently and so transform his relationship to power, what I read rhetorically as a shift in Saul's *res* and *verba*. Just as Saul's understanding of the source of true power suddenly changes from himself to God, so too does the repetition and amplification of pride in the play shift to the repetition and amplification of humility. This transition is seen most readily in the soldiers, who, while certainly still in competition with each other, now compete not over physical destruction (persecuting Christians) but over physical preservation (saving Saul):

SAULUS: Oh mercyfull God, what aylyth me?
I am lame, my leggys be take me fro!
My syght lykewyse, I may nott see!
I can nott tell whither to goo!
My men hath forsake me also.
Whether shall I wynde, or whether shall I pas?
Lord, I beseche the, helpe me of thy grace!

PRIMUS MILES: Syr, we be here to help the in þi need—
Wyth all our affyance we wyll nott sessel!

SAULUS: Than in Damask I pray yow me lede
I[n] Godys name, accordyng to my promyse.

SECONDUS MILES: To put forth yowur hand, loke ye dresse.
Cum on your way! We shall yow bryng
Into þe cyte wythowt taryng. (197–210)

That the soldiers do not abandon Saul but rather support him in his moment of physical need signals an important reconfiguration of the soldiers' competitive service: the soldiers now redirect their efforts to work together. This change in their behavior signals a shift in the delivery of *pathos*; for, it is no longer only about how Saul's behavior affects characters in the play but how it affects the audience members as well: "the specific…details of Saul's plight exist to stir and involve the audience."[19] By enabling the audience to invest emotionally in Saul's conversion, the playwright redirects the *pathos* achieved by *amplificatio* towards the audience. Indeed, once the soldiers have found a room for Saul, their rhetorical amplification by Accumulation participates in God's plan for Saul, magnifying the miracle Saul underwent by repeating and reinforcing its wonder *to the audience*:

PRIMUS MILES: I maruayle gretly what yt doth mene,
To se owur master in thys hard stounde!
The wonder grett lyhtys þat were so shene
Smett hym doune of hys hors to þe grownde,
And me thowt that I hard a sounde
Of won spekyng wyth voyce delectable,
Whych was to [vs] wonderfull myrable.

SECONDUS MILES: Sertenly thys ly3t was ferefull to see!
The sperkys of fyre were very feruent!
Yt inflamyd so greuosely about þe countre,
That, by my trowth, I went we shuld a bene brent!
But now, serys, lett vs relente
Agayne to Caypha and Anna, to tell þis chaunce,
How yt befell to vs thys greuauns. (248–61)

Working together not only to help Saul but also to spread God's miraculous actions, the first and second soldiers effectively become rhetoricians announcing Saul's new found identity and humility in the play, with both soldiers amplifying the new topic, or *res*, of Saul's conversion through their *verba*: each speaks of the lightening (250, 254–57) and the first soldier also speaks about the sound of God's voice (251–53).[20] Their evangelizing role continues in the play's third station when the soldiers announce virtually the same message to Caiaphas and Anna (367–80), a repetition that anticipates and further magnifies the humility that the final station of the play will explore through its presentation of Saul as preacher. In spite of their rhetorical function, however, the soldiers themselves do not acquire the humility that Saul does; rather, they remain servants to the high priests and continue Saul's initial mission of persecuting Christians by pursuing him as convert. This important fact confirms *amplificatio*'s primary role in delivering the play's didactic message, because once the interpretation of humility begins, the playwright redirects *amplificatio*'s end goal of *pathos* towards the audience for the remainder of the play.

Although the play's third station foregrounds Saul's humility, humility in the play does not initially stem from Saul as pride did; rather, the source of the play's humility is Ananias, the priest who baptizes and teaches Saul. Ananias obediently responds to God's call, despite his own personal reservations:

ANANIAS: Lord, I am aferd, for aluay in my mynd
I here so myche of hys furyous cruelte,
Þat for spekyng of þi name to deth he will put me.

DEUS: Nay, Ananie, nay; I assure þe
He wulbe glad of thy cummyng! (224–28)

Ananias already possess the fear that Saul has to acquire, and despite his fear, Ananias proves himself a truly obedient servant, unlike Saul's soldiers who return to the high priests' employ.

As *amplificatio* informed Saul's pride and humility in the first and second stations respectively, so too do its techniques inform the sermon Saul delivers in the third station. Dressed in "dyscyplys wede" (stage direction after 502) and preaching, Saul's *verba* (costume/props and language) are again consistent with his *res*—the topic of his conversion. (During the second station when Saul converted, his costume still represented his former pride while his words suggested his new-found humility.) Any disjunction in Saul's character is now squashed as Saul's visual and verbal markers realign, a reality that the opening lines of Saul's sermon convey by recasting the opening lines of the play to focus on God's power instead of Saul's: "The Lord þat ys shaper of see and of sonde, / And hath wrowȝt wyth hys worde al thyng at hys wyl, /...send me soch speech þat I the truth say" (502–03, 506).[21] Saul states that he is only a conduit in God's larger plan, graciously acknowledging his servitude to the Lord (this inverts Saul's relation to power in the first station where he used his service to Caiaphas and Anna to bolster his own status and power). A fully developed and realized thematic sermon,[22] Saul's sermon also employs *amplificatio* by reminding the audience that humility opposes and is the antidote for pride; furthermore, it draws on his own earlier experience to illustrate pride and humility: "Whoso in pryde beryth hym to hye, / Wyth mysheff shalbe mekyd as I mak mensyon" (523–24). The development of Saul's sermon therefore sticks closely to Robert of Basevorn's advice for preachers: "[t]he third method of Amplification is by reasoning or argumentation, which in preaching occurs especially in three ways," the third of which "is by example" because it "avails much with lay people who are pleased with examples. The Apostles and other saints passed to the kingdom of God through many tribulations, therefore we ought to also."[23] The trials and tribulations that Saul undergoes in the play are made into the examples that his sermon teaches the audience, and, in addition to himself, Saul also uses Christ as an example of humility: "'Lern at myself, for I am meke in hart'— / Owur Lorde to hys seruantys thus he sayth, / 'For meknes I sufferyd a spere at my hart'" (537–39). Through these examples, Saul "presents himself as an *exemplum* of *imitatio Christi*: just as he imitates Christ by humbling himself, so will his auditors imitate Christ if they do the same."[24] What is more, Saul's "description of [the Seven Deadly Sins] is rendered immediate and personal by his identification with, and of, the audience; when, for instance, he notes that pride 'often dystroyeth both most and lest,' he recalls his earlier characterization of the audience and urges them to consider the sin in their own lives."[25] The emotional persuasion of the audience begun in Saul's conversion finds its completion in the message of his sermon, where Saul asks audience members to "empty their bodies of 'synne and folye' (530) as he has."[26] Saul's sermon models both the humility and the imitation of humility that is intrinsic to being a good Christian, and in the process, attempts to persuade audience members through a rhetorically motivated emotional connection to act in this way in their own lives.

Part III: Saul's Emotional Impact

The playwright reinforces the veracity of Saul's humility after his sermon ends, as Saul humbly accepts the consequence of his conversion:

> SERUUS SACERDOTUM: To Anna and Caypha ye must make your recurse.
> Com on your way, and make no delacyon!
>
> SAULUS: I wyll yow succede, for better or wors,
> To the pryncys of prystys wyth all delectacyon! (587–90)

Modeling the behavior Saul learned from Ananias, Saul agrees to follow the servant despite the physical harm that doing so may entail, a harm that Anna confirms in desiring to bring Saul to death (613). Saul's obedience confirms his trust in the Lord and also leads to his safe deliverance, as Poeta relates it, in a basket (652): Saul's "submission to the divine will takes precedence over the mere mechanics of his escape and forces the audience to internalize the same spiritual lesson which [Saul's] story as a whole has portrayed. For by not showing [Saul's] escape, the dramatist implicitly asks the spectators to make the same leap of faith in God's providence that [Saul], in his words and deeds, has already accomplished."[27] Saul's ability to amplify his experience and make it relatable reveals how the play models a humility that is imitable. The hymn with which the play ends similarly reinforces and amplifies the humility that Saul's sermon teaches, working emotionally on the audience as the sermon and escape do: "The hymn, which possibly the whole audience is invited to sing, ends the drama on a note of solemn devotion" that "construes the audience's proper response to their new, internalized perception of God's providential plan."[28] If the play were staged in various locations, walking between them in a procession would also model the behavior of Saul's sin, conversion, and humility for the audience members by forcing them to physically experience the *pathos* of the journey. This message is not dependent on the play's staging, however, as my production in the round clarified: Saul's rhetoric, and in particular his and the playwright's use of *amplificatio* throughout, effectively communicate the *pathos* of Saul's journey and initiate the audience into his emotional experience.

Amplificatio offers a rhetorical method to track and catalogue Saul's changing relationship to pride and humility throughout the play. The playwright's use of *amplificatio* enhances the emotion—pride or humility—that Saul experiences pre- and post-conversion and teaches the audience how to internalize lessons of penance and humility. Just as the *Conversion of St. Paul* models the rhetorical redirection of its titular character from sinful bombast to humble sermon, so too does it make the emotional means to rectify forgone behavior accessible to any audience member.

Notes

1. This production of *St. Paul* was staged in the round as a dinner theatre. F.J. Furnivall argued that the play was staged on pageant wagons in the Introduction to his edition of the play: *The Digby Plays with an Incomplete 'Morality' of Wisdom, Who is Christ*, EETS es 70 (London: Oxford University Press, 1896). In more recent years, scholars have contested Furnivall's interpretation, arguing instead for a place-and-scaffold model of performance. See Mary del Villar, "The Staging of *The Conversion of St. Paul*," *Theatre Notebook* 25 (1970–71): 64-68; Glynne Wickham, "The Staging of Saint Plays in England," in *The Medieval Drama*, ed. Sandra Sticco (Albany: State University of New York Press, 1972) 99–119; and Raymond J. Pentzell, "The Medieval Theatre in the Streets," *Theatre Survey* 14 (1973): 1–21, doi.org/10.1017/s0040557400005020.
2. I have written elsewhere about *St. Paul's* engagement with the thematic sermon and how Saul's evolving relationship with the play's emcee Poeta enables the rhetorical practice of *inventio*, or invention, to unfold. See Ann Hubert, "Preaching Rhetorical Invention: Poeta and Paul in the Digby *Conversion of St. Paul*," *Early Theatre* 18 (2015): 9–32.
3. Sources from Antiquity that discuss *amplificatio* include Cicero's *De Inventione* 1:100–05 and De Oratore 2.312–32 & 3.104–07; the *Rhetorica ad Herennium* 2:47–49; and Quintilian's *Institutio Oratoria* 4.2.70, 6.2.24–36, 8.4, & 9.2.104. For discussions of *amplificatio's* use in medieval sermons, see chapters 39 and 40 of Robert of Basevorn, "The Form of Preaching," trans. Leopold Krul O.S.B., in *Three Medieval Rhetorical Arts*, edited by James J. Murphy (Berkeley: University of California Press, 1971); and Chapter 20 of Ranulph Higden, *Ars componendi sermones*, translated by Margaret Jennings and Sally A. Wilson, in *Dallas Medieval Texts and Translations* 2, edited by Philipp W. Rosemann (Paris: Peeters, 2003). For an overview of amplificatio in sermon literature, see Siegfried Wenzel, *Medieval Artes Praedicandi: A Synthesis of Scholastic Sermon Structure* (Toronto: The University of Toronto Press, 2015) 80–84.
4. Heinrich Lausberg, *Handbook of Literary Rhetoric: A Foundation for Literary Study*, translated by Matthew T. Bliss, Annemiek Jansen, and David E. Orton, edited by David E. Orton and R. Dean Andersen (Brill: Leiden, 1998) 118.
5. Lausberg 113. "Quint. *Inst.* 8.pr.6 *orationem…omnem constare rebus et verbis.*"
6. Quintilian, *The Orator's Education Books 6–8*, edited and translated by Donald A. Russell, *Loeb Classical Library 126* (Cambridge, MA: Harvard University Press, 2001) 393. The original Latin can be found at 8.4.3 and reads as follows: "Quattor tamen maxime generibus video constare amplificationem, incremento comparatione ratiocination congerie" (392). Quintilian discusses the four types of amplification at length in 8.4 of *The Orator's Education*. See pages 391–407 in Russell's *Loeb* edition for this discussion.
7. Quintilian 57. The original Latin can be found at 6.2.23–24 and reads as follows: "Interim notasse contentus sum, non id solum agere adfectus, ut quae sunt ostendantur acerba ac luctuosa, sed etiam ut quae toleranda haberi solent, gravia videantur, ut cum in maledicto plus iniuriae quam in manu, in infamia plus

poenae dicimus quam in morte. Namque in hoc eloquentiae vis est, ut iudicem non in id tantum compellat, in quod ipsa rei natura ducetur, sed aut qui non est aut maiorem quam est faciat adfectum" 56.

8. Cicero, *On the Ideal Orator*, translated by James M. May and Jakob Wisse (Oxford: Oxford University Press, 2001) 255–56. The original Latin can be found at 3.27.107 and reads: "alii vero ancipites disputationem, in quibus de universe genere in utramque partem disseri copiose licet" (Cicero, *De Oratore Book III*, translated by H. Rackham, *Loeb Classical Library* [Cambridge, MA: Harvard University Press, 1942] 84).
9. Krul 180.
10. Citations of the play are from Donald C. Baker, John L. Murphy, and Louis B. Hall, Jr., *The Late Religious Plays of Bodleian MSS Digby 133 and E Museo 160* (Oxford: Oxford University Press, 1982).
11. Russell 397–99.
12. The horse is "a traditional symbol of Saul's pride" (Victor I. Scherb, "Frame Structure in *The Conversion of St. Paul*," *Comparative Drama* 26:2 (1992): 124–39, here cited from 131). Linda Seidel explains that "the European representation of the rider became so charged with specific social reference that, around 1200, it could be employed as an image of Pride and could be presented…as a cautionary figure. The idea for the motif dates back to the late Roman Empire and Prudentius's epic poem, the *Psychomachia*" ("Early Medieval Images of the Horseman Re-Viewed," in *The Study of Chivalry*, edited by Howell Chickering and Thomas H. Seiler [Kalamazoo: Medieval Institute Publications, 1988] 390).
13. Chester N. Scoville, "The Hood and the Basket: Image and Word in the Digby *Conversion of St. Paul*," *Research Opportunities in Renaissance Drama* 41 (2002): 157–67, here cited from 158–59. Scoville also notes that the stable groom "is violating sumptuary legislation in his attempt at social climbing" and that "in aping the appearance of his betters identifies himself as a lawbreaker" (158) and as "a victim of inordinate pride" (159).
14. Scoville observes a similar phenomenon: "Although the Stabularius and Saul are of different classes, their statements amount to the same thing: an assertion of rank and authority, and a demand that others acknowledge their worthiness" ("The Hood," 158). Scoville goes on to discuss how the visual and verbal interact in the play but privileges the verbal over the visual where I argue for their interdependence. Scoville returns to these points in his book *Saints and the Audience in Middle English Biblical Drama* (Toronto: University of Toronto Press, 2004) 85–88.
15. The servant insults the stable groom by saying he looks like a horse—"Yf on loke yow in þe face þat neuer se yow ere, / Wuld think ye were at þe next dore by!" (94–95)—and by saying that his face is covered in dung: "Your face was bepayntyd wyth sowters code! / I sey neuer sych a syȝt, I make God a vow! / Ye were so begrymlyd and yt had bene a sowe!" (103–05). As Scoville explains, the first insult about the stable groom's face "will depend on the set, but since the scene takes place in or near a stable it is likely that 'þe next dore by' is a horse's stall, with a horse's posterior visible above the door" ("The Hood," 159). The stable groom's

work and the servant's insults connect both men to horses and so heighten their imitation of Saul and underscore the sin of pride from which they both suffer.

16. Russell 405–07.
17. Krul 180.
18. Scherb reads the stable groom scene as anticipating Saul's fall from his horse, when he too is "thrown into the mire" (131). For a detailed discussion of the relation between the stable groom scene and Saul's conversion and baptism, see Matthew C. Hansen, "Dancing in the Shadows: Ritual, Drama, and the Performance of Baptisms in the Digby *Conversion of St. Paul* and Philip Massinger's *The Renegado,*" *Quidditas* 30 (2009): 56–77.
19. Scoville, *Saints* 92.
20. For an excellent close reading of the soldiers' language and its assimilation of the disparate accounts of Saul's conversion in the Acts of the Apostles, see Chester N. Scoville, "On Bombshells and Faulty Assumptions: What the Digby *Conversion of Saint Paul* Really Did with the Acts of the Apostles," in *'Bring furth the pagants': Essays in Early English Drama Presented to Alexandra F. Johnston,* edited by David N. Klausner and Karen Sawyer Marsalek (Toronto: University of Toronto Press, 2007) 197–211, particularly 201–04.
21. Saul's sermon also includes several Latin biblical authorities which, Scoville notes, are themselves "a kind of verbal icon" (*Saints* 99), and so can be included as yet another *verba* marking Saul's humility.
22. Hubert 11–17.
23. Krul 181–82.
24. Hubert 22.
25. Scoville, *Saints* 101.
26. Hubert 22.
27. Scherb 135.
28. Scherb 135.

Kyd, Shakespeare, and Arden of Faversham: a (belated) reply to MacDonald Jackson

Brian Vickers

> The settlement of the authorship of *Arden* is perhaps the most important one to be achieved in the whole range of Elizabethan drama.[1]

So wrote the distinguished Australian attribution scholar, E. H. C. Oliphant, in 1926 (while arguing the case for Marlowe). At that time Kyd's authorship had been advocated in several journal articles. Although F. S. Boas, in the first attempt at a complete edition of Kyd's works, had not included *Arden of Faversham*, he listed it among plays that showed "incontestable evidence of his influence."[2] Fairly enough, Boas regarded the similarities that, up to that time, had been pointed out between it and *The Spanish Tragedy* as constituting insufficient evidence, but he recognized that the piece is, as a whole, too nakedly realistic, too free, as the Epilogue claims, from "filèd points" to be in his distinctive vein. Yet, in the cadence and diction of many passages, and in the combination of lyrically elaborate verse-structure with colloquial directness of speech, *Arden of Faversham* recalls the manner of Kyd far more nearly than that of Shakespeare, to whom it has been often groundlessly attributed. And one episode in it is palpably inspired by *The Spanish Tragedie.*[3] Boas referred to the bad dream of Michael, Arden's servant, who has been forced to betray his master to the assassins that Alice Arden and her lover Mosbie have hired to kill him. Michael's cry awakens Arden and his friend Francklin, whose words—"What dismal outcry calls me from my rest?"—closely match those of Hieronimo, woken by the death cry of his son Horatio. To Boas, the "imitation" of the earlier play "is so transparent that it is almost sufficient of itself to prove that Kyd could not have written the anonymous play." That deduction has been echoed in our time, but the opposite conclusion has also been reached.

Soon after Boas's edition appeared, scholars began to provide evidence of Kyd's hand in other plays. The pioneer was Charles Crawford, who in 1903 ascribed *Arden of Faversham* to him.[4] Crawford was a most diligent student of Elizabethan literature, with a great expertise in identifying anonymously-published work. Compiler of a *Concordance to Thomas Kyd* (1908), he produced an exemplary edition of the 1600 verse anthology *Englands Parnassus* (Oxford, 1913), while his copy of another verse anthology, *Bodenham's Belvedére* (1600), deposited in the British Library—interleaved and annotated with authorship attributions—remains an invaluable resource.[5] The next scholar to identify Kyd as author of *Arden of Faversham* was Walter Miksch, in his diligent doctoral dissertation (1907), supervised by that excellent scholar Gregor Sarrazin.[6] H. Dugdale Sykes joined the debate in a slighter essay first published in 1919.[7] Kyd's authorship was definitively confirmed in 1948, by a Danish scholar, P.V. Rubow, who supplied over 30 pages of documentation.[8] The collective evidence provided by these scholars, largely ignored since then, is so important that I have collected 50 matches from Crawford, 80 matches from Miksch, and 95 matches from Rubow on my website.[9] In his 1973 Revels edition M. L. Wine cited in his commentary a dozen "genuine" parallels that had been identified by these pioneers—he deserves special credit for including Rubow, otherwise ignored by Anglo-Saxon scholars, and added another 40 in an Appendix, in which he placed scare-quotes around the word "parallels."[10]

Wine's new scepticism about Kyd's authorship was due to him having read MacDonald Jackson's 1963 Oxford B. Litt. thesis, in which he rejected all claims made for Kyd's authorship of *Arden of Faversham* and argued that Shakespeare had written one scene, the quarrel between Alice Arden and her lover Mosby (scene 8 in Wise's edition).[11] For over fifty years Jackson has reiterated this position in a series of journal articles, most of them re-worked in a 2014 monograph, and has had the satisfaction of seeing the play included in the recently published *New Oxford Shakespeare*.[12]

But the reiteration of a thesis, however insistent, does not necessarily guarantee its correctness, and alternative interpretations are always possible. In 2007 I began investigating the three anonymously published plays that had been associated with Thomas Kyd and published a first draft of my findings the following year.[13] I had recently discovered anti-plagiarism software, a resource developed by universities to weed out student plagiarism which has enormous potential for attribution studies.[14] I use it not to study plagiarism as such, but to identify instances of a dramatist repeating himself, a phenomenon found throughout Renaissance drama but not yet properly recognized.[15] If two texts are uploaded into this software it automatically highlights every word-sequence (collocation) of any chosen length, from two words upwards, that occurs in both texts. The process is wholly objective, unaffected by a researcher's bias, and can be replicated by any other user, thus fulfilling two basic criteria of a scientific method. Attribution scholars in the pre-electronic era, however well-read and however extensive their memories, could never claim to have searched the whole of a literary work, objectively and systematically. Anti-plagiarism software allows us to do so as the first stage in identifying a potential candidate for the authorship of an anonymously published or co-authored work. I tested *Arden of Faversham* against each of Kyd's accepted plays, *The Spanish Tragedy* (1587), *Soliman and Perseda* (1588), and *Cornelia (*1594), translated from Robert Garnier's *Cornélie* (1579).[16] This produced a list of matching collocations, which I then manually checked, one by one, against a database of all plays performed in the public theatres for the period in question. Drawing on publicly available databases (LION/EEBO) I compiled a corpus of plays performed between 1579 and 1596 (Kyd died in 1594), which amounted to seventy-five plays. I uploaded it into InfoRapid Search and Replace, a freely available and highly efficient word-retrieval program devised by Ingo Straub.[17] I entered each matching collocation into this resource and in a fraction of a second could see whether it was a commonplace phrase or whether it matched the work of any particular author. If a sufficient number of unique matches between the target text and an author's authenticated work can be established, then a strong attribution can be made. Although I use a variety of linguistic approaches in my ongoing research, anti-plagiarism software has provided, in my judgment, an invaluable method for identifying authorial self-repetition.[18]

Having collected, and sifted, several hundred repeated phrases that occurred both in Kyd's three accepted plays and in the three anonymously published plays I had been investigating, I reached the conclusion that he was the sole author of *The True Chronicle History of King Leir, and his three daughters* (1589), *Arden of Faversham* (1590), and *Fair Em, The Millers Daughter of Manchester* (1590). It was only to be expected that, given his life-long part-attribution to Shakespeare, MacDonald Jackson would object to my attribution of *Arden of Faversham* and he did so in an essay for this journal, "New Research on the Dramatic Canon of Thomas Kyd."[19] To begin with, Jackson generously conceded the value of my approach: "Vickers...had the excellent idea of using plagiarism software to search pairs of plays for shared three-word phrases" (107). As he put it elsewhere, "plagiarism software...has the advantage over my *LION* searches of being mechanized, objective, and readily replicable."[20] Despite this praise, the burden of Jackson's 2008 essay was that my method "cannot be trusted" (107), that his critique had "exposed the weakness of [my] case for Kyd's authorship of *Arden of Faversham* and, indeed, for an "extended Kyd canon" (116). Jackson concluded that "Vickers's methodology is clearly inadequate to the task of supporting the proposed new attributions" (125).

In responding to Jacksons criticism, I will first deal with the question of verbal resemblances between *Arden* and Kyd's three accepted plays. In the second part of this essay I will introduce a complementary topic, new to this debate, concerning Kyd's dramaturgy in *Arden*, as compared with the three other plays.

I

In my original essay I described the process by which, having identified matching sequences of three or more words found in *Arden of Faversham* and in the three accepted plays, I checked against my database, retaining only the unique matches.[21] I then quoted about 40 of the most striking instances, many of which had been noticed by the pioneering scholars in the last century. Their method relied on repeated reading of the plays, note-taking, and a good memory for phrasal matches. This method, sometimes dismissed as hunting for "parallel passages," and misused by some practitioners, has been validated in our time, especially by the scholars who did so much to establish Middleton's canon: E. H. C. Oliphant, R. H. Barker, David Lake, MacDonald Jackson, and R. V. Holdsworth.[22] Commenting on the occurrence of the same two sentences in two Middleton plays, each time from the mouth of a character convinced of his own brilliance, Lake observed that the fact that "these two sentences occur, in close proximity, in a single scene in each play, is very strong evidence that one mind is responsible for both, for what we observe here is a sequence of verbal ideas retrieved intact by the memory of an author."[23]

These "verbal ideas" represent an interplay between character and situation in a new composition that sparks off in the dramatist's mind a reminiscence of an earlier one. Sometimes the context is similar, sometimes very different. A phrase might be innocuous in one situation; in another it can be sinister. Presenting matches in list form is acceptable but isolates them from their dramatic context, where they have an added significance. I shall briefly reconstruct the situations in which these examples occur in *Arden* and in Kyd's two tragedies. (Exact matches are printed in bold face; words and phrases underlined perform the same semantic or syntactic function in both passages.) In *Soliman and Perseda* the heroine, having seen the love-token that she gave her lover Erastus being worn by another woman (he had lost it), accuses him of deceit:

> Ah how thine eyes can **forge** alluring **lookes,**
> And faine deepe oathes **to wound** poore sillie maides (*SP* 857–59)

Perseda was mistaken but sincere: in *Arden of Faversham* Mosby is neither. We have heard him reveal in a soliloquy that he intends to get rid of Alice Arden once her husband is dead and he has got her money. When she appears and they start to quarrel, he accuses her of a Machiavellian dissimulation, assuming an appearance of distress in order to hurt him:

Ungentle Alice thy sorrow is my sore,
Thou knowst it wel, and tis thy pollicy,
To **forge** distressefull **looks, to wound** a breast (*AF* 8.55–57)

This is a striking parallel, both in vocabulary and sentence structure, stretching over two lines,[24] but Jackson has dismissed it three times over. In 1963 he claimed that Kyd's image is "characteristically confused." and that he "uses "forge" prosaically," to mean "contrive" or 'simulate," while in *Arden* "it retains a hint of a blacksmith's weapon-making."[25] Over a half-century Jackson has occasionally used subjective aesthetic judgments to dismiss Kyd's authorship, an approach that is out of place in modern attribution studies. The association between "forge" and a blacksmith is entirely of his own making, and it obscures the fact that the word "forge" has the same meaning in both contexts. In *Soliman and Perseda* Kyd pairs it with "faine," the feigning of false oaths, while in *Arden* it is paired with the false accusation of "policy," the trademark of deceivers, of whom Mosby is a supreme example. Despite Jackson's attempted association with blacksmiths, the two usages are identical.

We find similar contrasts between a sincere reaction and a feigned (or forged) one in these two plays. When Perseda sees Lucina wearing the necklace she had given Erastus, she experiences a sudden shock, as a bystander observes:

What ailes you, madam, that your colour changes?
—**A suddaine qualme**; I therefore take my leave. (*SP* 784–85)

Perseda's shock is genuine, but after Arden's murder Alice knows how to fake wifely concern when asked the same question:

What aile you woman, to crie so suddenly
—Ah neighbors **a sudden qualm** came over my hart
My husbands being foorth torments my mynde.
I know something's amisse, he is not well. (*AF* 14.301–04)

The two plays share longer phrasal sequences. In *Soliman and Perseda* Piston describes to Perseda the circumstances in which his master had killed Ferdinando. Erastus had managed to win back Perseda's chain from Lucina in a game of dice and was wearing the chain around his neck when they encountered Ferdinando, Lucina's lover:

Then Ferdinando **met** vs **on the way**,
And **reuild** my maister, saying he stole the chaine
With that **they drew**, & there Ferdinando had the prickado. (*SP* 1120–22)

Following this fatal encounter Erastus fled to Constantinople, leaving Perseda regretting her excessive anger and suspicion at the loss of the necklace:

> My hart had armd my tongue with **iniury**.
> To wrong my **friend, whose thoughts were** euer true (1131–32)

In *Arden of Faversham* Kyd repeated this situation of two men meeting in public, fighting with swords. After her plan to harm Arden in this way has failed, Alice tries to convince her husband that the brawl he has just had with Mosby was due to his misunderstanding their pretended jest:

> When we to welcome [thee][26] intended sport
> Came lovingly to **mete** thee **on thy way**,
> Thou **drewst** thy sword inraged with Jelousy,
> **And** hurte thy **freende**,
> **Whose thoughts were** free from harme. (*AF* 13.90–94)

The two sequences have in common the phrases "meet on the way," "drew(st) a sword," the matching verbs "wrong" and "harm," prefacing the tetragram (a four-word phrase) "friend whose thoughts were," and the synonymous adjectival phrases "ever true," "free from harm." Such co-occurrences far exceed the likelihood of having come about through chance or imitation. A few lines later Alice claims that it was Arden who started the brawl,

> after he had **revyled** [Mosby]
> By the **injuryous** name of perjurde beast (13.139–40)

Her speech supplies the two terms Kyd has used in his Turkish tragedy that were lacking here: "reviled" and "injury."

In both plays intrigue involves concealment and disapproval, real or feigned:

> **The rest** I dare not speake **it is** so **bad**. (*SP* 1995)
> And then conceale **the rest**, for **tis** too **bad** (*AF* 8.63)

The plotters' goal is the same, whether in Constantinople or Kent:

> To **send** them downe **to euerlasting night** (*SP* 2052)
> Arden **sent to everlasting night**. (*AF* 5.9)

In both plays Kyd uses a traditional image for a defenseless victim. When Soliman decides to have Erastus killed, he sends Brusor to bring him back from Cyprus.

Perseda realises that her supposed friend Lucina had been his accomplice:

> Lucina, came they husband to this end?
> To **leade a Lambe unto the slaughterhouse**. (*SP* 2139–40)

Michael, Arden's servant, having been forced to help the hired murderers' plot to kill his master, compares him to "the **Lambe**" who feeds 'securely on the down" while the "hunger bitten Woulfe orepryes his haunt" (*AF* 3.191–93). Suddenly he realises that he himself is now an accomplice in his master's destruction, and

> Do **lead thee** with a wicked fraudfull smile,
> As unsuspected, **to the slaughterhouse** (*AF* 3.201–02)

The quantity and quality of verbal matches between *Soliman and Perseda* and *Arden of Faversham* well justifies Charles Crawford's claim that Kyd's authorship of the latter could be settled from this play alone.

The Spanish Tragedy may contain slightly fewer close matches, but they include some striking parallels, none closer than the two night-scenes. As Horatio is being strangled, Bel-Imperia's cries—"Murder, murder, helpe Hieronimo helpe" (2.4.62)—bring Hieronimo on to the stage, "*in his shirt*," as the stage direction records, with this famous exclamation:

> **What outcries** pluck **me from my** naked bed
> And chill my throbbing hart with trembling feare (*Sp.T* 2.5.1–2)

In the final scene of the tragedy, having exacted his revenge, Hieronimo looks back to that horrible event, when Lorenzo and his accomplices "butchered up my boy, / In darke cruell night," shifting to the present tense to convey the persistent immediacy of the event:

> He shrikes, I heard, and yet **me thinks I heare**,
> His **dismall out-cry** eccho in the aire (*Sp.T* 4.4.108–09)

Kyd recalled this scene in *Arden of Faversham* when Arden's servant Michael has "**a fearefull dreame**," in which he imagines the hired murderers hunting him down after the murder:

> **Me thinks I heare** them aske where Michaell is
> And pittiless black Will, cryes stab the slave.
> The Pesant will detect the Tragedy. (*AF* 4.78–80)

Michael cries out in his sleep "ah Master Francklin helpe," rousing both Franklin and Arden:

> *Fran.* **What dismall outcry** cals **me from my** rest?
> *Ard.* What hath occasioned such a **fearefull cry**? (*AF* 4.87–88)

Kyd echoed the murder scene from *The Spanish Tragedy* at another point in *Arden of Faversham*. Hieronimo exclaims over his son's corpse:

> O poore Horatio, **what hadst thou misdoone?**
> To leese **thy life** ere life was new begun (*Sp.T* 2.5.28–29)

Michael expresses the same pity and regret as he realizes that the hired murderers have made him their accomplice in his master's murder:

> Ah harmeles Arden, how, how **hast thou misdone**,
> That thus **thy** gentle **lyfe** is leveld at (*AF* 3.195–96)

The aftermath of murder takes the same course in both plays. Hieronimo urges Pedringano, about to be hanged, to

> **Confesse** thy folly **and** repent thy **fault** (*Sp.T* 3.6.26)

The Mayor confronts Alice Arden with her husband's corpse and urges her to

> **Confesse** this foule **fault, and** be penitent (*AF* 16.2)

Pedringano, gulled into believing that he will be pardoned, had admitted Serberine's murder, so Hieronimo orders his execution:

> Dispatch, the faults approved and confest,
> **And by** our **law** he is **condemnd to die** (*Sp.T* 3.6.38–39)

Pedringano deserves his fate, but in *Arden* Bradshaw is in fact innocent, having only delivered a letter,[27] yet he suffers the same fate:

> **And** I am **by** the **law condemnd to die** (*AF* 18.3)

In *The Spanish Tragedy*, Alexandro, unjustly accused, abandons hope of better fortune:

Tis **Heaven is my hope.**
As for the **earth** it is too much infect,
To yeeld me **hope** of any of her mould. (*Sp.T* 3.1.35–37)

In *Arden* Susan expresses the same sentiment:

Seing no **hope** on **earth**, in **heaven is my hope**. (*AF* 18.36)

These extended matches, stretching to six identical words and corresponding prosodic placing, go far beyond the usual explanations, imitation or influence, and point to the same authorial memory drawing on its lexicon of phraseology.[28] Although Kyd translated *Cornelia* from the French, his individual "phraseognomy" (to adopt an attractive word created by John Sinclair)[29] can be seen, and it contains several unique matches. Altogether, more than 200 matching collocations between *Arden of Faversham* and Kyd's accepted canon have been identified. In recent research, testing Jackson's claim that Shakespeare wrote the Quarrel scene, in which he could only find 8 matching collocations with Kyd, I identified over 70.[30]

That summary shows selected results of my claim for Kyd's authorship of *Arden of Faversham* based on matching phraseology. As briefly mentioned, the burden of Jackson's 2008 essay was that my method "cannot be trusted" (107). He made four objections:

1. "we cannot evaluate these findings without knowing how many sequences of three or more words are shared between each of the anonymous plays ...and individual plays by Marlowe, Shakespeare, Peele, Greene, Lodge, Porter, Wilson, and others...Vickers has entered Kyd in a one-horse race, which Kyd cannot fail to win" (108). Had I compared *Arden* with Marlowe's plays, Jackson stated, I would have found "a residue of unique matches to Marlowe" (109).

2. Jackson claimed that *Arden* has more unique matches with *2 Henry VI* and *The Taming of the Shrew* than with any play by Kyd (110–16).

3. Although ignoring 39 of the 40 Kyd matches that I quoted, Jackson cited just one to claim that Shakespeare may perhaps have "echoed" it (118–19).

4. Jackson statistically re-interpreted the "raw" data that I supplied for the total matches between *Arden* and Kyd's plays to claim that the plays I ascribe to Kyd are "utterly different" from the accepted canon (119–25). Jackson

concluded that "Vickers's methodology is clearly inadequate to the task of supporting the proposed new attributions" (125).

This seemed like a damning dismissal of my methods, but closer examination reveals several serious flaws.

1. The short answer to Jackson's "one-horse race" objection is that over my scholarly career I have acquired enough knowledge of Elizabethan drama to be able to exclude those dramatists as having had significantly different linguistic and stylistic characteristics, not to mention dramaturgy (see below). I can cite a previous advocate of Kyd's authorship who reached the same position. Charles Crawford wrote in 1903 that, after "an exhaustive and painstaking examination of Kyd's work as a whole," he had concluded that "the vocabulary, phrasing, and general style" of the play "are those of Kyd, and that they cannot be mistaken for those of any other author of the time."[31] I am confident that individual searches in any of the other dramatists that Jackson mentioned—"Marlowe, Shakespeare, Peele, Greene, Lodge, Porter, Wilson, and others"—will find no-one who can shake the high probability that Kyd wrote *Arden of Faversham*. In fact, despite invoking so many other names, Jackson has repeatedly acknowledged that Marlowe and Kyd are the only two likely authors of the play, so it would be otiose to consider the others.[32] In his 2008 essay he singled out Marlowe as a test case:

> Had Vickers suspected in advance that the anonymous plays were by Marlowe, let us say, he would have run the software program to compare each of them in turn with canonical Marlowe plays and would have obtained lists of triples that differed from the list formed when the anonymous plays were compared with the canonical Kyd plays. And it is certain that when the resultant lists were checked against the 75-play database, a residue of unique matches to Marlowe would have survived. (109)

Such a test is indeed possible, but some Marlowe plays exclude themselves. The diction of *Tamburlaine the Great*, both parts, is distinct from most Elizabethan plays and, indeed, from anything he subsequently wrote. The chances of it sharing "unique matches" with *Arden* are remote. As for the other Marlowe plays, three of them—*Dido, The Massacre at Paris, Dr Faustus*—have highly unreliable texts. *Edward II* might seem a suitable candidate for comparison, and Jackson himself offered a list of eleven "unique parallels" between Kyd's *Soliman and Perseda* and *Edward II* (116–18), partly taken from Alfred Hart's classic book on Shakespeare's Bad Quartos.[33] According to Jackson, Hart had shown that "a dozen plays of the late 1580s or early 1590s—by Shakespeare, Marlowe, Kyd, and Peele—are interconnected by sharing the substance of 5 whole lines" (116). While some of these echoes may be due to actors' involuntary reminiscence, others are certainly evidence of authorial borrowing. Yet, although Jackson cited Hart's work, he failed to report Hart's scathing conclusion concerning *Edward II*, which he described as "the mystery play of this period" (376). Hart summed up his discussion in Table XXI, "Totals of lines common to paired plays named" showing that *Edward II* shares 5 lines with *Arden of Faversham*, 7 with *Soliman and Perseda*, 2 with *The Spanish Tragedy*, and 29 lines with other plays (383). Where Tucker Brooke had claimed that "Marlowe was prone to the repetition of striking lines and phrases" of his own earlier plays, amounting to 37 lines in *Edward II,* Hart pointed out that this did not

> account for 22 lines and passages "conveyed"—to use Pistol's term—from *Arden*, *Spanish Tragedy*, *Soliman and Perseda*, and *A Knacke to know a knave*, all of them acted or in print when he was writing his play, and [Peele's] *Edward I*. Marlowe's petty borrowings in *Edward II* total in all 65 lines, or two and a half percent of the length of the play. This amount of plagiarism exceeds anything found in the most corrupt play of that period and must equal what is present in *Wily Beguiled* (388).

Hart's singling out of Edward II as a play that re-used shreds and patches of plays performed on the London stage between 1587 and 1592 negates Jackson's argument that the links between Arden of Faversham and Kyd's plays are commonplace features of that period in Elizabethan drama.

In assessing Marlowe's debts to other plays, the question of chronology is essential. Wiggins dates Kyd's Turkish tragedy to 1588, *Arden* to 1590, and *Edward II* to 1592, a date that other Marlowe scholars would endorse.[34] Whereas traditionally, Marlowe's greater profile as a dramatist led scholars to see any verbal matches between his plays and Kyd's as proving the latter's indebtedness, ninety years ago that great scholar E. H. C. Oliphant (much admired by Jackson), objected to the automatic assumption that every parallel between *Arden of Faversham* and *Edward II* "is treated as plagiarism by Kyd from Marlowe," when the opposite could be the case.[35] Indeed, I have recently argued that Marlowe was in fact the borrower.[36] In that essay, following a close analysis of these texts, I have listed 58 unique matching collocations which *Edward II* took from *Soliman and Perseda* (60–63), and 76 "conveyed" from *Arden of Faversham* (63–68). We can thus reject MacDonald Jackson's claim that, if such a comparison were to be performed, "it is certain that...a residue of unique matches to Marlowe would have survived."

2. Jackson's persistent ignoring of chronology is particularly damaging for his second claim in "New Research on the Dramatic Canon of Thomas Kyd," that *Arden* has more unique matches with *2 Henry VI* and *The Taming of the Shrew* than with any play by Kyd. Using the LION database and an earlier version of WCopyfind, Jackson cited 51 unique matches with *2 Henry VI*, whereas, by his criteria for admitting parallels, there were a mere "21 unique matches between *Arden* and *The Spanish Tragedy*, 29 between *Arden* and *Soliman and Perseda*, and 4 between *Arden* and *Cornelia*" (110–14). He then performed the same procedure on Shakespeare's *The Taming of the Shrew* (114–16), identifying 44 unique matches. Jackson concluded that because "two early Shakespeare plays each have more matches with *Arden* than do any of Kyd's three canonical plays," his findings 'surely expose the weakness of Vickers's case" (116).

In effect, the parallels that Jackson cited with these "two early Shakespeare plays" should have been taken as supporting two hypotheses: either

(A) "Shakespeare wrote *Arden of Faversham*"; or
(B) "Shakespeare remembered the play well, from public performances."[37]

For over half a century of working on this play, Jackson has simply ignored the second hypothesis, together with the crucial questions of dating and chronology. In 1963 he dated *Arden of Faversham* to 1588–92, a sensible time-span, which he has recently narrowed to 1588–91.[38] In his authoritative chronology Martin Wiggins assigns *Arden* to 1590, thus antedating both *2 Henry VI* (1591) and *The Taming of the Shrew* (1592).[39] In his recent monograph Jackson listed the plays that, from his searches of LION, have most links to the *Arden* quarrel scene. The list, headed by *3 Henry VI* (1591), includes 17 other Shakespeare plays, sole and co-authored, performed before 1600. Jackson acknowledged in passing that "it is probable that no Shakespeare play tabled above was written before *Arden of Faversham*," without dwelling on its significance.[40] In other words, all the Shakespeare matches that Jackson claims are from plays post-dating *Arden*. In authorship attribution studies, such matches would normally be dismissed as likely due to imitation or influence, as in hypothesis B above. Remarkably, as throughout the last fifty years, Jackson failed to draw the inescapable consequences of this fact: Shakespeare cannot have been its author. The matches that Jackson collects with Shakespeare are indeed significant, since they show the degree to which he was influenced by Kyd, as several scholars have noted (a topic that deserves a full study). But they prove nothing about his authorship of this play.

Once we observe chronology we will see the difference between originator and imitator (whether deliberate or inadvertent). A proper side-by-side comparison between *The Spanish Tragedy* (1587), *Soliman and Perseda* (1588), *King Leir* (1589),[41] *Arden of Faversham* (1590), *Fair Em* (1591) and *Cornelia* (1594), shows that a dense network of individual linguistic choices, in the form of matching word strings from three to seven words long links these six plays, with additional significant parallels to Kyd's *The Housholders Philosophie*.[42] They all derive from the same lexicon of words and phrases. In Kyd's Turkish tragedy, Piston dismisses the braggart soldier Basilisco:

> Take **the** bra**ginst knaue in christendom** with thee (*SP* 399)

Arden uses the same phrasing to dismiss a suitor he has wronged:

> It is **the** ray**lingest knave in christendome** (*AF* 13.84)

Shakespeare must have been impressed by this formulation, for he re-used and varied it on four occasions:

1591	*2 Henry VI*: "the lying'st knave in Christendom" (2.1.24)
1592	*The Shrew*: "the lying'st knave in Christendom" (Ind. 2.24)
1591	*3 Henry VI*: "he is the bluntest wooer in Christendom" (3.2.83)
1592	*The Shrew*: "Kate the prettiest Kate in Christendom" (2.1.187)

We can conclude that the dramatist who wrote *Arden of Faversham* (1590) also wrote *The Spanish Tragedy* (c.1587; published 1592), and *Soliman and Perseda* (1589; published 1592). Neither of those plays had been published in 1590, hence the more than a hundred close verbal parallels that they share with Arden can only be explained by common authorship.

3. Jackson's third objection to my attributing *Arden* to Kyd was based on a highly selective consideration of the evidence that had been assembled since 1903. I had quoted some forty matching collocations, too many and too detailed to be the result either of imitation or coincidence. When a case has been made, and is then disputed, it is always significant to note which points the disputer discusses, and which he avoids. MacDonald Jackson simply ignored nearly all the matching phrases, a decision that can be interpreted either as a sign of complete confidence in his own thesis, or as a deliberate ignoring of inconvenient evidence (of which much more is now available). He picked out only one of them, that between the utterances of two men disturbed in the night:

What outcries pluck **me from my** naked bed (*Sp. T.* 2.5.1)
What dismall **outcry** cals **me from my** rest? (*AF* 4.87)[43]

I had argued that this parallel is "neither an allusion, nor a parody, but another instance of Kyd's self-plagiarizing." Jackson, however, only having quoted part of the extensive matches (discussed above) objected: "But this is mere assertion. It is just as likely that the author of *Arden of Faversham* remembered Kyd's unforgettable line."[44] If this were an isolated case of phrasal parallels, that comment might be justified, but in the context of the forty unique matches that I quoted, Jackson's rejection of this one seems an instance of "cherry picking," choosing the instance that suits your case and ignoring the rest of the evidence.

4. The fourth and last of Jackson's objections to my essay ascribing *Arden of Faversham* to Kyd involved statistics but was misguided. I had placed on my institute's website two tables: the first recorded the total number of matching three-word collocations between the canonical and newly-ascribed Kyd plays before checking against other plays performed between 1580 and 1596. In this process I whittled down the initial total of 419 matching collocations with *The Spanish Tragedy* to 32 unique matches; the 447 matches with *Soliman and Perseda* came down to 36; for *Cornelia* 164 matches reduced to 8. The second table contained the number of unique matches that remained. I attached no significance to the first table, since the number of common-place phrases that a play may share with the larger corpus can be affected by many factors, and I included it merely to show my careful procedure in eliminating all but unique phrases. Jackson, however, decided to calculate "the percentage of unique matches among total matches," and by using a series of statistical processes he proved, to his own satisfaction, that the canonical Kyd plays were "utterly different" from those that I had newly attributed (119–24). Jackson is celebrated for his knowledge of statistics; however, as is generally appreciated, statistics is a flexible tool and different users can achieve different results from the same data. Jackson's computations were based purely on irrelevant evidence, the "raw" data—the numerical totals of un-sifted matches, not on the specific parallels unique to Kyd that I had identified.

Fortunately, a genuine statistical analysis of my claims for an enlarged Kyd canon, made by examining the plays themselves, soon appeared. It came from an unexpected source, Professor Martin Mueller (Northwestern University). Mueller, a classical scholar with a separate qualification in Renaissance English Literature, had long been interested in "the problem of repetitive or formulaic language in the *Iliad* and *Odyssey*," to study which he developed a remarkable skill in digitally assisted text analysis.[45] Mueller was jointly responsible for creating the wonderful Chicago Homer website, an interactive resource that allows users to search all instances of verbal repetition in early Greek epic, from the famous "Homeric formulae" to the more extended repetitions that mark the transition from an oral to a written culture.[46] Mueller subsequently developed a similar resource for English drama, a database called "Shakespeare His Contemporaries," to consist of 600 non-Shakespearian early modern plays, marked-up to permit the identification of all repeated phrases. In August 2009 Professor Mueller posted two pieces on his blog ("*DATA. Digitally Assisted Text Analysis*") responding to my *TLS* essay. Having had many years' first-hand experience of working with repeated collocations, Mueller decided to test my claims for Kyd. He designed an experiment on 318 early modern plays, taken from the EEBO–TCP database, which included most of the surviving plays of the playwrights who wrote or began writing before 1642. This corpus had been linguistically annotated with a tagging procedure that allowed Mueller to extract all the word-strings, or n-grams, as they are known in Corpus Linguistics, extending from two words (a bigram) to seven words (a heptagram) that were repeated at least once; this yielded over a million repetitions and eight million occurrences.[47] Mueller then computed "the distribution of n-grams that are shared by two plays of the same author," from which it emerged that two plays by the same author generally share about twice as many unique n-grams as two plays by different authors. Of these 2,303 two-play combinations, 28 occur in the seven plays I attributed to Kyd, and, more significantly, "six place in the top quartile for shared two-play n-grams by the same author." In the first post he reached a provisional conclusion:

> On balance, my figures lend support to Vickers's argument although they are not conclusive. There are many plays by different authors that share more n-grams than the plays in the putative Kyd canon. On the other hand, if you play a ranking game with each play in the Kyd canon and list the plays with which it shares the most n-grams, some of the other "Kyd" plays will appear in the top five. Something is going on here.

Mueller returned to this issue a week later, evidently determined to devise a more searching test. As he ruefully noted, "authorship arguments provide huge yawns in English departments. But, as Vickers argued in his *TLS* piece, there is good reason to look with interest at an expanded Kyd canon. Shakespeare and Marlowe suddenly acquire a slightly older and gifted contemporary whose oeuvre has some size and considerable thematic and generic range."[48] In this second assay Mueller presented his new "corroborative evidence," having applied "discriminant analysis to lemma trigrams that occur at least 500 times in 318 early modern plays. There are 56 of them, and they range from *I will not* (2332 occurrences) to *what do you* (508). Riveting fragments of speech, but remarkably informative when you look at their distribution." He reported that, "Based on some tests with common trigrams I think they provide compelling corroborative evidence that Vickers is right about the *Leir* play, *Fair Em*, and *Arden*."

> Vickers made his argument for an expanded Kyd corpus on the basis of shared rare repetitions. In the old *Leir* play, *Fair Em*, and *Arden*, there are a lot of phrases that occur in the *Spanish Tragedy*, *Soliman and Perseda*, and the translation of *Cornelia*, but nowhere else. My test ignores this evidence and looks instead at the most common trigrams, which show up in at least half (164) or more than 90% (297) of all plays. Vickers's and my conclusions therefore rest on an entirely different evidentiary basis. To the extent that we agree, the case is greatly strengthened: the evidence of rare and of common phenomena support each other.
>
> Now to Kyd. I assigned to Kyd all plays that Vickers assigns to him, except for *1 Henry VI*, because Vickers assigns parts of it to Shakespeare. And I added the "prequel", *The first part of Jeronimo* because it shares a lot of rare repetitions with the *Spanish Tragedy*, although it shares relatively few rare repetitions with the other plays in the Kyd canon.

In Mueller's test *I Jeronimo* scored only 30 percent, while *Cornelia* scored 80 percent, which shows how much of Kyd's linguistic idiom has permeated this translation. The remaining results of Mueller's discriminant analysis were as follows:

> *Soliman and Perseda* (85.3%)
> *The Spanish Tragedy* (96.1%)
> *Arden of Faversham* (97.4%)
> *The true chronicle history of King Leir* (99.3%)
> *Fair Em* (99.5%)

As Mueller commented,

> These are striking results. First, Discriminant Analysis rejects the prequel as Kyd's. It assigns it to the grab bag of anonymous plays with a 57.4% chance. So it is not fooled by the presence of many shared repetitions between it and *The Spanish Tragedy*. Secondly, Discriminant Analysis very strongly confirms that the other plays come from the same stable. Indeed, if *The Spanish Tragedy* is the clearest case of a play by Kyd, the three English plays are, so to speak, a little more Catholic than the Pope. If you combine my evidence from common trigrams with Vickers's evidence from rare shared repetitions, you would have to be very skeptical about the power of quantitative analysis not

to acknowledge the fact that the claim for an expanded Kyd canon rests on quite solid evidence.

Mueller's judgment was independently endorsed by Dr Albert Yang, one of a trio of medical researchers at Harvard Medical School who have developed sophisticated digital methods to analyse such problems as arrhythmia (irregular heart beat). They have adapted their methodology for the digital analysis of literary texts, developing an algorithm that uses all the words of a text (unlike most practitioners of stylometry, who rely on selected word-classes), and have applied their methods successfully to texts in both English and Chinese.[49] In 2009 they received the Calvin Hoffman Prize, awarded annually for the best study of Marlowe, for an essay on "Marlowe and the History Play," which showed that he did *not* write Shakespeare's history plays.[50] In 2017 I asked Dr Yang to perform a similar analysis of the canons of Shakespeare and Kyd. His results showed that the three plays I newly ascribe to Kyd (*King Leir*, *Arden of Faversham*, and *Fair Em*), together with the three accepted plays (*The Spanish Tragedy*, *Soliman and Perseda*, and *Cornelia*), appear together as a homogeneous group, clearly differentiated from Shakespeare. The results of these varied tests, both manual and digital, strongly suggest that Kyd wrote *Arden of Faversham*.

II

In addition to the deep affinity between *Arden of Faversham* and Kyd's three accepted plays at the level of phraseology, it also shares significant features of his dramaturgy. In my *TLS* essay I briefly referred to three of these, "intrigue, the vengeful woman, and black comedy" (p. 13). As other scholars have pointed out, Kyd is the first master of intrigue plots in English drama. Gregor Sarrazin, comparing Kyd's dramaturgy with that of his contemporaries, observed that *The Spanish Tragedy* is better constructed than any play of Greene's, and surpasses most of Marlowe's tragedies in this respect.

> In Kyd especially we find a greater unity of plot, a stronger focus of interest upon fewer characters. More than any of his contemporaries, Kyd's tragedies may be called tragedies of intrigue. In this respect they recall Italian Renaissance tragedy. Shakespeare's *Hamlet* and *Othello* have a similar character.[51]

Madeleine Doran, in her outstanding synthesis of Renaissance theories of drama and the English response to a European tradition, divided Elizabethan tragedy into "three main types, according to theme and pattern: *De casibus* tragedy, or the fall of the mighty, with ambition as a chief motivating force; Italianate intrigue tragedy, with love or jealousy usually the central passion; and domestic tragedy, or the tragedy of crime in the lives of ordinary citizens."[52] Kyd has strong claim to have initiated not only the second of these genres, in *The Spanish Tragedy*,[53] but also the third, in *Arden of Faversham*.[54] Both plays are structured around crimes of passion. In the Spanish play Lorenzo has Horatio killed so that Balthazar can satisfy his desire for Bel-Imperia, Horatio's beloved. Lorenzo employs two subordinates to do the deed, Pedringano and Serberine, then uses one to murder the other, promising Pedringano a pardon. In a soliloquy he explains his Machiavellian plot:

> Thus must we worke that will avoide distrust,
> Thus must we practise to prevent mishap,
> And thus one ill, another must expulse. (3.2.105–07)

As for his accomplices, who have "for coine their soules endangered," Lorenzo dismisses them contemptuously:

> They that for coine their soules endangered
> To save my life, for coyne shall venture theirs:
> And better 'tis that base companions dye,
> Than by their life to hazard our good haps.
> Nor shall they live, for me to feare their faith:
> Ile trust my selfe, my selfe shalbe my freend,
> For dye they shall, slaves are ordeind to no other end. (115–19)

In Kyd's Kentish tragedy, Mosbie, joint plotter with Alice Arden, his mistress, to murder her husband, reveals in a soliloquy that he plans the same fate for his accomplices:

> Then, Arden, perish thou by that decree,
> For Greene doth eare the land and weede thee up
> To make my harvest nothing but pure corne.
> And for his paines Ile heave him up a while
> And after smother him to have his waxe.
> Such bees as Greene, must never live to sting.
> Then is there Michael and the painter too,
> Chief actors to Ardens overthrow:
> Who when they shall see me sit in Ardens seat,
> They will insult upon me for my meed
> Or fright me by detecting of his end.
> Ile none of that, for I can cast a bone,

To make these curres pluck out each others throat;
And then am I sole ruler of mine owne. (8.23–36)

But Mosbie is even more ruthless than Lorenzo, for he includes among the accomplices of whom he must rid himself the woman he claims to love, who is ready to sacrifice everything for his sake:

Yes mistres Arden lives; but she's my selfe,
And holy Church rites makes us two, but one.
But what for that I may not trust you Alice,
You have supplanted Arden for my sake,
And will extirpen me to plant another:
Tis feareful sleeping in a serpents bed.
And I will cleanely rid my hands of her.
Here enters Alice.
But here she comes and I must flatter her. (8.37–44)

The intrigue in *The Spanish Tragedy* is far more intricate, involving several plot levels, but *Arden* shares many other features with it, as a full analysis could show.

The second element of dramaturgy common to both plays is the use of comedy in a life threatening situation. Lorenzo gets Pedringano to kill the other accomplice by promising to issue him a pardon, to be brought to his trial by a Page. Disobeying orders, the Page opens the box and finds it empty, a situation that Kyd brings to life in the boy's prose soliloquy:

By my bare honesty, heeres nothing but the bare emptie box: were it not sin against secrecie, I would say it were a peece of gentlemanlike knavery. I must go to Pedringano, and tell him his pardon is in this boxe, nay, I would have sworne it, had I not seene the contrary. I cannot choose but smile to thinke, how the villain wil flout the gallowes, scorne the audience, and descant on the hangman, and al presuming of his pardon from hence. Will't not be an odde jest, for me to stand and grace every jest he makes, pointing my finger at this boxe: as who would say, "Mock on, heeres thy warrant." Is't not a scurvie jest, that a man should jest himself to death? Alas, poore Pedringano, I am in a sorte sorrie for thee, but if I should be hanged with thee, I cannot weep. [*Exit.* (3.5.6–19)

The execution scene is brilliantly staged, with more surprises. Pedringano enters "*with a letter in his hand, bound,*" and expresses his relief that the Page boy has at last come from Lorenzo with the pardon. Confident that his life will be spared, Pedringano confesses his crime to the Lord Marshal, Hieronimo, in verse (3.6.28–32), descending to prose to abuse the Hangman. Indeed, Pedringano shows outrageous arrogance in jesting with the Hangman, as it must seem to everyone present—except the audience, and the Boy holding the empty box. The joke is on Pedringano, however, after Hieronimo has left the courtroom in disgust at his impudence, ordering the execution to take place:

PEDRINGANO: Nay soft, no haste.
DEPUTY: Why, wherefore stay you, have you hope of life?
PEDRINGANO: Why aye.
HANGMAN: As how?
PEDRINGANO: Why Rascall by my pardon from the King.
HANGMAN: Stand you on that, then you shall off with this. (3.6.99–104)

And the hangman "*turnes him off*" in full view of the audience. As Arthur Freeman observed, "the hangman's contemptuous reply to the prisoner's hope of pardon...implies that at this point the boy has finally thrown open the box and revealed it quite empty".[55] But Pedringano has the last laugh, for the letter he carries, exposing Lorenzo as the instigator of Horatio's murder, is delivered to Hieronimo, inspiring his comprehensive revenge.

The Kentish tragedy's plot came from Holinshed's *Chronicles* (1587), which described how Thomas Arden was killed only after a sequence of failed attempts, and our playwright saw the comic possibilities of these blunders.[56] The source gave him the names of Black Will and Shakebag, the "two desperat ruffins" hired for the murder. Black Will was evidently a comic attraction, for a villainous character with the same name recurs in another play of this period.[57] He is introduced to us with a mixed comic-vicious descent, "such a slave, so vile a rogue," a former soldier who "played such pranckes | As all the Campe feard him for his villany" (2.5–10)—where "pranckes" is a euphemism for more serious offences. When Greene approaches him about the killing, Will's bloodthirsty language promises much: "Give me the money, and Ile stab him as he stands pissing against a wall, but Ile kill him...My fingers itches to be at the peasant" (2.97–8, 105). A few moments later (in theatre time) their first opportunity presents itself, as Greene points out their prey, Arden having been walking a turn in St Paul's, a common rendezvous for business deals. But the churchyard of St Paul's was also lined with booksellers' stalls, and just as Will is preparing to "run [Arden] through," a printer's apprentice, wanting to prevent pilfering when the crowd comes out of the cathedral, shuts the stall:

[*Then lets he down his window, and it breaks Black Will's head*
WILL: Zounds, draw, Shakebag, draw! I am almost kiled.

PRENTICE: Wele tame you, I warrant.
WILL: Zounds, I am tame enough already. (3.50–54)

Will's self-deflating reply shows the comic nature of his role, as the audience laughs both with and at him. The would-be murderer is foiled by a banal accident, the harmer is harmed: "my broken head greeves me not so much, as by this meanes Arden hath escaped" (64–66). This setback (the dramatist's invention, not in Holinshed) is the first of Will and Shakebag's many failures to carry out their "hit." Will's utterances are terrifying—

Seest thou this goare that cleaveth to my face?
From hence ne'er will I wash this bloody staine,
Till Arden's hart be panting in my hand (3.104–06)

but after another six bungled attempts we begin to doubt whether he and Shakebag will ever succeed. When they do so in the final scene, comic expectations are reversed, in a mixture of disgust with the killers and sympathy for the victim.

The third element of Kyd's dramaturgy that links *The Spanish Tragedy*—and *Soliman and Perseda*—with *Arden of Faversham* is the presence of a vengeful woman. Renaissance theories of womanhood did not include such savage attributes as a readiness for physical violence and murder.[58] Lady Macbeth has to invoke a supernatural power to suspend her female qualities (they do so, but only for a while):

Come you spirits
That tend on mortal thoughts, unsex me here,
And fill me from the crown to the toe, top-full
Of direst cruelty. (1.5.40–43)

Kyd's heroines need no such licence, as we see from Bel-Imperia. Earlier in the play, when she has learned from Horatio how her beloved Andrea was murdered by Balthazar, she feels closer to Horatio, only to question her feelings:

But how can love find harbour in my brest,
Till I revenge the death of my beloved.
Yes, second love shall further my revenge.
Ile love Horatio my Andreas freend,
The more to spight the Prince that wrought his end. (1.4.65–68)

The audience may well have forgotten Bel-Imperia's desire for revenge, but Kyd re-introduces it at a crucial stage in the plot. We see her in a soliloquy chafing at Hieronimo's inaction: "why art thou so slacke in thy reuenge?" (3.9.7–11), and when she finally confronts him, Kyd gives her a lengthy tirade in which she upbraids Hieronimo for not having revenged Horatio's death (4.1.1–29). Accusing him of forgetfulness and "Ingratitude unto thy Sonne," she vows to take revenge herself, if need be:

For here I sweare in sight of heaven and earth,
Shouldst thou neglect the love thou shouldst retaine,
And give it ouer and devise no more,
My selfe should send their hatefull soules to hel,
That wrought his downfall with extreamest death.

As a woman in a man's world there would be little chance of her doing so openly, but Kyd's brilliant idea of having Hieronimo mount the tragedy of *Soliman and Perseda* allows Bel-Imperia to do just that. Bel-Imperia impersonates Perseda, whose beloved Erastus has been murdered by the tyrant Soliman, a role for which Balthazar is perfectly suited. At the play's climax, Erastus (Lorenzo) is murdered by the Marshall (Hieronimo) on Soliman's command. Perseda, as a woman, seems to accept her powerlessness, since Soliman still ("Yet") rules:

Yet by thy power thou thinkest to command,
And to thy power Perseda doth obey:
But were she able, thus she would revenge
Thy treacheries on thee ignoble Prince: *Stab him.*
And on herselfe she would be thus revengd *Stab herselfe.* (4.4.63–67)

An Elizabethan audience would have accepted that the conditional mood is appropriate for a woman unable to take direct physical revenge for herself, so they must have been shocked when Bel-Imperia broke that taboo. If her killing Balthasar was a surprise to the audience, her killing herself surprised Hieronimo, since it was not in his script. As he explains to the stunned spectators,

For though the story saith she should have died,
Yet I of kindness, and of care to her,
Did otherwise determine of her end.
But love of him whom they did hate too much,
Did urge her resolution to be such. (141–45)

In Bel-Imperia's "resolution" reality and fiction intersect, in the high style appropriate to the "stately written Tragedie" that Kyd devised. Alice Arden's surroundings are anything but stately, yet she is motivated by the same spirit of anger that drove Bel-Imperia. In her first soliloquy she expresses her wish that "some ayrie spirit" might throw her husband into the sea, for

> Sweet Mosbie is the man that hath my hart;
> And he usurpes it, having nought but this,
> That I am tyed to him by marriage.
> Love is a God and marriage is but words,
> And therefore Mosbie's title is the best.
> Tush! Whether it be or no, he shall be mine,
> In spight of him, of Hymen, and of rytes. (1.93–104)

Alice sophistically rejects the sacrament of marriage as "but words," describes her husband as a "usurper," and transfers that "title" to her lover on no authority but her own. (As we discover, both Alice and Mosbie describe their status as adulterous murderers in the most favourable light.) Her hope that Arden might die by the intermediary of a spirit soon gives way to a wish to be personally involved in his death, along with Mosbie: "did we not both | Decree, to murder Arden in the night?" (1.192–93). Alice acknowledges her dependence on her lover: "Yet nothing could inforce me to the deed | But Mosbie's love" (1.272–73), but plans to be jointly responsible: "Weele have him murdered as he walkes the streets" (1.441–43). As their hired murderers commit one blunder after another, Alice proposes a "new device" (12.65), that they should pick a quarrel with Arden in the street, which the murderers can exploit. That plot having also misfired, Alice is almost ready to do the murder herself, as she tells Mosbie, wounded in the abortive brawl:

> for, when I saw thee hurt,
> I could have toke the weapon thou letst fall,
> And runne at Arden, for I have sworne,
> That these mine eyes, offended with his sight,
> Shall never close, til Arden's be shut up.
> This night I rose and walkt about the chamber,
> And twice or thrice, I thought to have murthred him.
> MOSBIE: What, in the night? Then had we been undone! (14.81–88)

The thought of a wife walking around the bedroom ready to kill her husband would be shocking anywhere, but especially in Elizabethan London. The "complot" that Mosbie has now laid requires the help of Black Will, whom Alice woos with a mixture of sexuality and money (a fee of £10). Alice even expresses her readiness to help in the murder, but Shakebag's conventional notion that women are "too faint-hearted" makes him stick to the notion of murder as an exclusively male activity:

ALICE:	Here would I stay, and still encourage you, But that I know how resolute you are.
SHAKEBAG:	Tush! You are too faint harted, we must do it.
ALICE:	But Mosbie will be there, whose very lookes Will ad unwonted courage to my thought, And make me the first that shall adventure on him.
WILL:	Tush, get you gone! 'Tis we must do the deede. (14.134–40)

Alice finally gets her wish, becoming if not "the first" to venture on Arden, then not far behind. The conspirators lure Arden into a game "at tables," his back to Black Will, who, on the cue words, pinions him from behind:

MOSBIE:	Ah, Master Arden, "Now I can take you." [*Then Will pulles him down with a towell.*]
ARDEN:	Mosbie! Michael! Alice! What will you do?
WILL:	Nothing but take you up, sir, nothing els.
MOSBIE:	There's for the pressing iron[59] you tould me of. [*He stabs Arden.*]
SHAKEBAG:	And ther's for the ten pound in my sleeve. [*He stabs him.*]
ALICE:	What, grones thou?—Nay, then give me the weapon!— Take this for hindring Mosbie's love and mine. [*She stabs him.*]
MICHAEL:	O, mistres! (14. 232–39)

Although we have long been aware of Alice's hatred for her husband, it still comes as a shock when she stabs him. Arden's pathetic exclamation—"Mosbie! Michael! Alice! What will you do?"—is echoed by Michael's shocked, or incredulous words, "O, mistres!" In having her revenge on the man who has hindered "Mosbie's love and mine," Alice Arden declares her identity with Bel-Imperia, who stabs the man who killed her lover, and with Perseda, who stabs the woman who betrayed her husband to his death. Alice's urgent demand, "Nay, then give me the weapon!" echoes Perseda's, in the play written two years earlier, when she revenges herself on the woman who had betrayed her husband: "give me the dagger then" (5.3.49). All three women were the creation of Thomas Kyd.

In a recent essay affirming his belief that Shakespeare wrote "the middle scenes of the play", MacDonald Jackson commented on my review of his book *Determining the Shakespeare Canon.*[60]

> Turning to *Arden of Faversham*, Vickers notes similarities in wording and dramatic organization that link the Quarrel Scene to the rest of the quarto text and concludes that "Whoever wrote scene 8 wrote the rest of the play". *On the basis* of *some dramaturgical likenesses* and "multiple verbal matches" that he and a succession of previous scholars have found between *Arden* and the Kyd canon (especially *Soliman and Perseda*), he repeats his claim that the sole author of the domestic tragedy was Kyd. He asserts that "Jackson's dismissal of Kyd as author of *Arden*, fifty years ago, has excused him from further acquaintance with his plays". This is not true. Rereading *The Spanish Tragedy*, *Soliman and Perseda*, and *Cornelia* many times has simply led me to different conclusions regarding *Arden* from those at which Vickers has arrived.[61]

It is disappointing that Jackson has not read those plays with fresh eyes, and perhaps it was unrealistic to expect him to view them differently. But his statement that my ascription rests on the basis of "some dramaturgical likenesses" shows his failure to respond to the new evidence I have cited. Far from mere likenesses, the fact is that the three main elements I have singled out determine the whole dramatic structure of *Arden*, and they are demonstrably the creation of Thomas Kyd. No other Elizabethan play contains all three, and the deep identity they share with his other tragedies proves that we can now give him the credit for having written *Arden of Faversham*.[62]

Notes

1. E. H. C. Oliphant, "Marlowe's Hand in *Arden of Faversham*," New Criterion 4 (1926): 76–93 (77).
2. *The Works of Thomas Kyd, edited from the original texts* (Oxford, 1901); 2nd edition, with minor changes (Oxford: The Clarendon Press, 1955) xxxix.
3. *Works of Thomas Kyd* lxxxix–xc.
4. See "The Authorship of *Arden of Faversham*," *Jahrbuch der Deutschen Shakespeare-Gesellschaft* 39 (1903): 74–86; reprinted in Crawford, *Collectanea, 1st Series* (Stratford-on-Avon: Shakespeare Head pr., 1906) 101–30.
5. Lukas Erne is currently preparing a scholarly edition of this text for Cambridge University Press.
6. *Die Verfasserschaft des Arden of Feversham* (Breslau, 1907) 83.
7. "Arden of Feversham," *Sidelights on Shakespeare* (Stratford-on-Avon, 1919) 48–76.
8. P.V. Rubow, *Shakespeare og hans Samtigide* (Copenhagen, 1948) 108–16, 120–44. I am grateful to Dr. Lene Petersen, of the University of Southern Denmark (Odense) for providing me with translations of relevant passages in this little-known work studying "Shakespeare and his Contemporaries." Fortunately, Rubow quotes the texts in English.

9. See www.brianvickers.uk/?page_id=808, and my essay, "Kyd's authorship of *Arden of Faversham*: admissible evidence, 1903–2018"(forthcoming).
10. See M. L. Wine, ed., *The Tragedy of Master Arden of Faversham* (London: Methuen, 1973) passim, and Appendix I, "Parallels in *Arden of Faversham*," 141–48.
11. See M. P. Jackson, "Material for an edition of *Arden of Faversham*" (B. Litt. thesis, Oxford University, 1963).
12. See Jackson, "Shakespearean features of the poetic style of *Arden of Faversham*," *Archiv für das Studium der neuren Sprachen und Literaturen* 230 (1993): 273–304; "Shakespeare and the quarrel scene in *Arden of Faversham*," *Shakespeare Quarterly* 57 (2006): 249–93; "Compound adjectives in *Arden of Faversham*," *Notes and Queries* 53 (March, 2006): 51–55; "Parallels and poetry: Shakespeare, Kyd, and *Arden of Faversham*," *Medieval and Renaissance Drama in England* 23 (2010): 17–33; "Gentle Shakespeare and the authorship of *Arden of Faversham*," The *Shakespearian International Yearbook* 11 (2011): 25–40; "Reviewing authorship studies of Shakespeare and his contemporaries, and the case of *Arden of Faversham*," *Memoria di Shakespeare*, Nuova serie 8 (2012): 149–67; *Determining the Shakespeare Canon.* Arden of Faversham *and* A Lover's Complaint (Oxford: Oxford University Press, 2014) 1–126, 219–44; "*Arden of Faversham* and Shakespeare's Early Collaborations: The Evidence of Meter," *Style* 50 (2016): 65–79. He has contributed three essays touching on *Arden* to Gary Taylor and Gabriel Egan, eds., *The New Oxford Shakespeare Authorship Companion* (Oxford, 2017): "One-Horse Races: Some Recent Studies," 48–59; "Shakespeare, *Arden of Faversham*, and *A Lover's Complaint.* A Review of Reviews," 123–35; and "A supplementary Lexical Test for *Arden of Faversham*," 182–193.
13. See Brian Vickers, "Thomas Kyd, secret sharer," *Times Literary Supplement*, 18 April 2008, 13–15. This is now available on my website: www.brianvickers.uk/wp-content/uploads/2016/05/Vickers-Thomas-Kyd-The-Secret-Sharer.pdf
14. I originally used "Pl@giarism," devised by Dr Georges Span for the Law Faculty of Maastricht University, which is no longer supported. An admirable replacement is "WCopyFind," produced by Dr Lou Bloomfield of the University of Virginia; see plagiarism.bloomfieldmedia.com/z-wordpress/software/wcopyfind/
15. See Brian Vickers, ed., *The Collected Works of John Ford. Vol. II* (Oxford: Oxford UP, 2016), Introduction 2, "Identifying Co-Authors," 33–75, especially "Dramatists repeat themselves," 44–75.
16. All dates are from Martin Wiggins and Catherine Richardson, *British Drama, 1533–1642: A Catalogue*, 10 Vols. (Oxford, 2012–). (I should like to record my personal conviction that *The Spanish Tragedy* dates from around 1585.) References are to the following texts: *Arden of Faversham 1592*, ed. H. Macdonald (Oxford: Malone Society Reprints, 1940), with line-references from *The Tragedy of Master Arden of Faversham*, ed. M. L. Wine (London: Methuen, 1973); *The Spanish Tragedy 1592*, ed. W. W. Greg (Oxford: Malone Society Reprints, 1948), with line-references from The Spanish Tragedy, ed. Philip Edwards (London: Methuen, 1959); *Soliman and Perseda* [*1592/93*], ed. Lukas Erne (Oxford: Malone Society Reprints, 2014).
17. See www.inforapid.de/html/searchreplace.htm.

18. See, e.g., Brian Vickers, "Shakespeare and Authorship Studies in the Twenty-First Century," *Shakespeare Quarterly* 62 (2011): 106-42; "Identifying Shakespeare's Additions to *The Spanish Tragedy* (1602): A New(er) Approach," *Shakespeare* 8 (2012): 13–43. Brian Vickers, "The Two Authors of *Edward III*," *Shakespeare Survey* 67 (2014): 102–19; "Giving Greene his *Groatsworth*," *Papers of the Bibliographical Society of America*, forthcoming.
19. *Research Opportunities in Medieval and Renaissance Drama* 47 (2008): 107–27 (107).
20. Private communication 18 April 2008. In a recent essay on Shakespeare's supposed presence in *Cardenio* Jackson himself made use of "plagiarism software in authorship studies, as pioneered by Brian Vickers," finding matching collocations between Theobald's *Double Falsehood* and two Fletcher plays. See Jackson, "Looking for Shakespeare in Double Falsehood: Stylistic Evidence," in David Carnegie and Gary Taylor, eds., *The Quest for Cardenio: Shakespeare, Cervantes, and the Lost Play* (Oxford: Oxford UP, 2012) 160–1.
21. Since then I have performed a fresh search with WCopyfind and found additional unique matches, more than 50 with *The Spanish Tragedy*, and over 40 with *Soliman and Perseda*. I have yet to extend my search using the powerful new resource released by Pervez Rizvi in October 2017, a database of 527 early modern plays which he has marked up so as to allow the identification of all instances of verbal repetition; see www.shakespearestext.com/Collocations and N-Grams
22. For a discussion of the legitimate use of verbal parallels, see Brian Vickers, *Shakespeare, Co-Author. A Historical Study of Five Collaborative Plays* (Oxford: Oxford UP, 2002) 60–67.
23. See Vickers, *Shakespeare, Co-Author* 64–5 and Lake, *The Canon of Thomas Middleton's Plays* (Cambridge: Cambridge University Press, 1975) 147.
24. As Martin Mueller has pointed out, the chances of any other writer producing the words "forge," "looks," and "to wound," in that order must be rather low (personal correspondence, 7 April 2018).
25. Jackson, "Material," 101–2; "Quarrel" 282 n.; *Determining the Shakespeare Canon*, 96–97 and 225 n.
26. Wine's emendation; Quarto reads "thy."
27. Holinshed added a marginal gloss: "*Bradshaw as unjustlie accused, as his simplicitie was shamefully abused*," explaining that there had been a "misunderstanding of the words contained in the letter" (ed. Wine 158).
28. For further examples of Kyd's self-repetition in *Arden*, see Darren Freebury-Jones, "A raven for a dove": Kyd, Shakespeare, and the Authorship of *Arden of Faversham*'s Quarrel Scene," *Archiv fur das Studium der neueren Sprachen und Literatur* 253 (2016): 39–64.
29. See his essay, "Phraseognomy," in Sinclair, *Trust the Text. Language, corpus and discourse* (London: Routledge, 2004) 177–84.
30. See Brian Vickers, "Is EEBO (LION) suitable for attribution studies?" *Early Modern Literary Studies*, forthcoming.
31. Crawford, "The Authorship of *Arden of Faversham*," *Jahrbuch der Deutschen Shakespeare Gesellschaft* 39 (1903): 74–86, quoted from Crawford, *Collectanea, 1st Series* 101–30 (113,118).

32. In the preface to his 1963 thesis Jackson offered this foretaste of his findings: "I show that the various arguments in favour of Kyd's or Marlowe's responsibility for *Arden* are virtually worthless," before devoting over 30 pages to rejecting Kyd ("Material," iii, 72–3, 92–115). He has repeated this bracketing of the two dramatists several times, most recently in 2014: "Apart from Shakespeare, the main contenders for the authorship of *Arden of Faversham* have been Thomas Kyd and Christopher Marlowe." See *Determining the Shakespeare canon* 2, 15–16, 47–48, 63, 79, 83, 110–11, 113–14.
33. See Hart, *Stolne and Surreptitious Copies: A Comparative Study of Shakespeare's Bad Quartos* (Melbourne, 1942), who cited parallels linking *Edward II* with *Arden of Faversham* (368), *Soliman and Perseda* (368–69), and T*he Spanish Tragedy* (369). I have been instrumental in persuading Melbourne University Press to reissue Hart's pioneering book: see the 2016 reprint, ISBN 9780522871029 052287102X.
34. H. B. Charlton and R. D. Waller, in their edition of *Edward II* (London: Methuen, 1933) 5–27, assigned it to "the period 1591–3," with December 1592 as the likely date of its performance. Charles R. Forker, in his edition, *Edward the Second* (Manchester: Manchester UP, 1994) 14–17, placed it in 1591–2. Martin Wiggins dates it 1592.
35. Oliphant, "Marlowe's Hand" 81ff.
36. See Brian Vickers, "Marlowe in *Edward II*: Lender or Borrower?" in Joseph Candido, ed., *The Text, the Play, and the Globe: Essays on Literary Influence in Shakespeare's World and His Work in Honor of Charles R. Forker* (Lanham, MD: Farleigh Dickinson UP, 2016) 43–74.
37. Some scholars have argued that Shakespeare's reminiscences are so frequent that he may have acted in it, a possibility that Jackson has always vehemently denied. See Darren Freebury-Jones, "Kyd and Shakespeare: Authorship versus Influence," *Authorship* 6.1 (2017): 1–24 www.authorship.ugent.be/article/view/4833
38. See "Material" 65-78; *Determining the Shakespeare Canon* 15.
39. Wiggins, *British Drama 1533–1642: A Catalogue. Volume III: 1590–1597* (Oxford: Oxford UP, 2013) 9, 92, 155.
40. *Determining the Shakespeare Canon* 21, 23.
41. See Brian Vickers, "Kyd's authorship of King Leir," *Studies in Philology* 115 (2018): 433–71.
42. See Brian Vickers, *Recovering Thomas Kyd: a canon restored* (forthcoming).
43. In 1903 Charles Crawford noted another partial parallel, Soliman's exclamation, "What dismall Planets guides this fatall hower?" (*SP* 652).
44. "New Research" 118. Jackson repeated this retort in later versions of this essay, most recently in the 2017 *Authorship Companion* 133.
45. See his Hilda Hulme Memorial Lecture, given at London University in July 2013: "Shakespeare His Contemporaries: collaborative curation and exploration of Early Modern drama in a digital environment," *Digital Humanities Quarterly* 8.3, at www.digitalhumanities.org/dhq/vol/8/3/index.html, paragraph 11.
46. See homer.library.northwestern.edu, Ahuvia Kahane and Martin Mueller, eds.

47. See Mueller's blog, DATA (Digitally Assisted Text Analysis) 18 August 2009, "N-grams and the Kyd canon: a crude test," available at www.brianvickers.uk/wp-content/uploads/2016/05/Martin-Mueller-on-Brian-Vickers-and-the-Kyd-canon.pdf
48. See Mueller, DATA blog of 23 August 2009, "Vickers is right about Kyd," available on the same website.
49. See Yang et al., "Information categorization approach to literary authorship disputes," *Physica* A 329 (2003): 473–83 (474). They demonstrated the validity of their method with impressive analyses of the classic 18th century Chinese novel, *The Dream of the Red Chamber*, which exists in a damaged manuscript containing the work of two authors; the *Federalist* Papers, jointly written by Alexander Hamilton and James Madison; and *The Two Noble Kinsmen*, co-authored by Shakespeare and Fletcher.
50. See Yang et al., www.psynetresearch.org/uploads/7/5/8/1/7581337/hoffman_essay.pdf
51. Gregor Sarrazin, *Thomas Kyd und sein Kreis. Eine litterarhistorische Untersuchung* (Berlin, 1892) 66 (my translation).
52. Doran, *Endeavors of Art: A study of form in Elizabethan drama* (Madison: U of Wisconsin P, 1954) 115. Alfred Harbage also emphasized the "historical importance of Kyd's *Spanish Tragedy*" in this respect: see "Intrigue in Elizabethan Tragedy," in Richard Hosley, ed., *Essays on Shakespeare and Elizabethan Drama in honour of Hardin Craig* (London: Routledge and K. Paul, 1963) 37–44 (37).
53. All quotations are from W.W. Greg, ed., *The Spanish Tragedy (1592)*, (Oxford: Malone Society Reprints, 1949), but with act, scene and line references to Philip Edwards, ed., *The Spanish Tragedy* (London: Methuen, 1959).
54. All quotations are from Hugh Macdonald, ed., *Arden of Faversham 1592* (Oxford: Malone Society Reprints, 1947), but with scene and line references to M.L. Wine, ed., *The Tragedy of Master Arden of Faversham* (London: Methuen, 1973).
55. Freeman, p. 117.
56. Wine reprints the source in his edition, 148–59.
57. Samuel Rowley, *When You See Me, You know Me*; cf. Wine, ed. xlvi.
58. See, e.g., Ian Maclean, *The Renaissance Notion of Woman* (Cambridge: Cambridge UP, 1980).
59. Alluding to an earlier confrontation, in which Arden had removed Mosbie's sword, claiming that, as an artisan (a tailor), he had no right to wear it and should rather carry "your bodkin, | Your Spanish needle, and your pressing Iron" (1.310–13). In the source Mosbie strikes Arden with the iron, which would be a heavy, and a risky weapon to use on stage.
60. See Brian Vickers "No Shakespeare to be Found," *Times Literary Supplement*, 24 April 2015, 9–11 (11). (The title was supplied by an editor.)
61. See Jackson, "Shakespeare, *Arden of Faversham*, and *A Lover's Complaint*. A Review of Reviews," in Gary Taylor and Gabriel Egan, eds., *The New Oxford Shakespeare Authorship Companion* (Oxford: Oxford UP, 2017) 123–35 (132), my italics.
62. Among recent studies of Kyd, see the following by Darren Freebury-Jones: "'Fearful Dreams' in Thomas Kyd's Restored Canon," *Digital Studies/le Champ*

Numérique 9.3 (2019), doi.org/10.16995/dscn.309; "Corresponding Stage Directions in Plays Attributable to Kyd," *ANQ* 32.1 (2019): 16–17, doi.org/10.1080/0895769X.2018.1457940; "In Defence of Kyd: Evaluating the Claim for Shakespeare's Part Authorship of *Arden of Faversham*," *Authorship* 7.2 (2018), doi.org/10.21825/aj.v7i2.9736; "Kyd and Shakespeare: Authorship versus Influence," *Authorship* 6.1 (2017); "Possible Light on the Authorship of *Fair Em*," *Notes and Queries* 64.2 (2017): 252–54; "The Diminution of Thomas Kyd," *Journal of Early Modern Studies* 8 (2019): 251–77; "Exploring Verbal Relations between *Arden of Faversham* and John Lyly's *Endymion*," *Renaissance and Reformation* 41.4 (forthcoming, 2019): 7–22. See also Pervez Rizvi, "Small Samples and the Perils of Authorship Attribution for Acts and Scenes," *ANQ* 30 (2018), doi.org/10.1080/0895769X.2018.1537841, which challenges one of the tests used by MacDonald P. Jackson to attribute scenes 4–9 of *Arden of Faversham* to Shakespeare. Jackson replied in "Reconsidering a Lexical Test of *Arden of Faversham*: A Response to a Critique," *Shakespeare* (2019), www.tandfonline.com/doi/full/10.1080/17450918.2019.1573847. See also Brian Vickers, "Verbal Repetition in *Arden of Faversham*: Shakespeare or Kyd?" *Notes and Queries* 65 (4): 498–502.

PGIL2020USA